Coaching YMCA Rookies Flag Football

YOUTH SUPER SPORTS™

We build strong kids, strong families, strong communities.

Library of Congress Cataloging-in-Publication Data

Coaching YMCA Rookies flag football / YMCA of the USA.
p. cm.
Includes bibliographical references.
ISBN 0-7360-3705-5
1. Flag football--Coaching. I. YMCA of the USA.

GV952.C62 2001
796.332'8--dc21 2001016876

ISBN: 0-7360-3705-5

Published for the YMCA of the USA by Human Kinetics Publishers, Inc.

The YMCA of the USA expresses its sincere appreciation to Charles T. Kuntzleman, EdD, Director, Fitness for Youth and Adjunct Associate Professor of Kinesiology, University of Michigan, Ann Arbor, for developing the Health and Fitness Circles for the YMCA Flag Football Program.

The YMCA of the USA also expresses its sincere thanks to the NFL Fund for financing the development of the flag football materials for the YMCA Youth Super Sports Program.

YMCA Project Coordinator: Richard Jones
Character Development Scale Developers: Maureen Weiss; Diane Whaley, PhD; Aaron Weintraub; Windee Weiss; and Emilio Ferrer-Caja
Project Writer: Bonnie Pettifor
Managing Editor: Coree Schutter
Assistant Editor: Scott Hawkins
Copyeditor: Lisa Morgan
Proofreader: Susan C. Hagan
Graphic Designer: Robert Reuther
Graphic Artist: Francine Hamerski
Photo Editor: Clark Brooks
Cover Designer: Jack W. Davis
Photographer (cover and interior): Tom Roberts
Illustrators: Tom Roberts (Mac art); Dick Flood (line drawings)
Printer: Versa Press

Printed in the United States of America 10 9 8 7 6 5 4 3 2 1

Copies of this book may be purchased from the YMCA Program Store, P.O. Box 5076, Champaign, IL 61825-5076, (800) 747-0089.

The YMCA of the USA does not operate or manage the YMCA Youth Super Sports Program or any of its components or facilities associated with the program.

Contents

Part I

The Job

Thank you for agreeing to be a coach in the YMCA Rookies program of YMCA Youth Super Sports. The job is challenging, but with effort and enthusiasm, you'll find it rewarding. In part I we'll tell you about YMCA Youth Super Sports, the best sports program in America. As we share with you our philosophy about children's sports programs in chapter 1, you'll see why we think YMCA Youth Super Sports is special. In chapter 2 we'll present you with your job description and request that you bring the YMCA philosophy to life as you teach flag football to your young players. Then in chapter 3 we'll describe what it is like to be a young child 4 to 7 years old (in case you've forgotten). This will give you a feel for what your players are capable of understanding and doing.

In chapter 4 we describe the way we want you to teach flag football to your players, what we call the "games approach." It's not the traditional way adults have taught sports to children, but you'll see why it is a better way—the YMCA way. It's essential that you understand and use this games approach to teaching YMCA Rookies flag football.

Our overall objectives in part I are to prepare you to do your job well and to impress upon you the potential influence you can have on the young people you coach. It's your chance to make a difference!

chapter

1

Welcome to YMCA Youth Super Sports

We're glad that you have decided to be a coach in the YMCA Youth Super Sports program. As a YMCA Rookies coach you will introduce a group of young people to the game of flag football. We ask you not only to teach them the basic skills and rules of the game but also to make learning the game a joyful experience for your players. You see, we want them to play the game not only this season but for many years to come. And we want you to have fun teaching them because we'd like you to help us again next season.

OK, let's get started. In this guide you'll find essential information about teaching flag football the YMCA way. In the next section we'll explain more about the best sports program in America—YMCA Youth Super Sports and especially the YMCA Rookies program, of which you'll be a part. Next is your job description for being a YMCA Rookies flag football coach, along with some reminders about how to work with 4- to 7-year-olds. Then we'll show you how to teach flag football using the games approach. We'll provide you with a season plan and a complete set of practice plans for 4- to 5-year-olds and another set for 6- to 7-year-olds. In the last part, we'll explain to you how to teach the four main components of the flag football season plan: skills and tactics, rules and traditions, fitness and safety, and character development. And throughout the book, Lucky, the YMCA Youth Super Sports mascot, will help illustrate key points. We hope that by seeing Lucky on these pages, you'll be reminded to keep the fun in your practices and games.

Please read the entire guide carefully and consult it regularly during the season. And if your YMCA offers you the opportunity to participate in a YMCA Rookies Flag Football Coaches Course, be there! The 3 1/2-hour course will help you use our games approach to teaching the game.

Let's begin by looking at what YMCA Youth Super Sports is, the YMCA's philosophy of youth sports, and the three parts of YMCA Youth Super Sports: YMCA Rookies, YMCA Winners, and YMCA Champions.

YMCA Youth Super Sports

We've named the program YMCA Youth Super Sports because we're confident it's the best-designed sport program available anywhere for young people ages 4 to 16. To design the program we brought together the research and knowledge of sport scientists who spend their careers studying children's sports and the practical wisdom of YMCA youth sports directors who guide literally millions of young people through sport programs. Our objective for YMCA Youth Super Sports is to help young people not only become better players, but also become better people. We recognize that not every child can win the contest, but every kid can be a winner in YMCA Youth Super Sports. That's why our motto for the program is "Building Winners for Life."

The YMCA triangle, representing spirit, mind, and body, is the inspiration for the YMCA Youth Super Sports program (see the triangle in figure 1.1). YMCA Youth Super Sports is currently designed for six sports: soccer, baseball, softball, basketball, volleyball, and flag football. These sports are available through three programs:

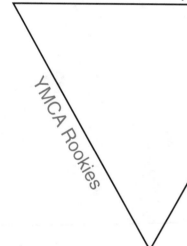

YMCA Rookies—a precompetitive, instructional program to teach 4- to 7-year-old girls and boys the basic skills and rules of the game.

YMCA Winners—the YMCA's unique, values-based sports program for young people ages 8 to 16.

YMCA Champions—an innovative opportunity for 8- to 16-year-olds to demonstrate personal achievement in and through sport.

Figure 1.1 YMCA Youth Super Sports triangle.

All three programs have been carefully crafted to maximize the potential for children to have a positive and beneficial experience under your leadership. Sport is not just frivolous games in children's lives; it influences them profoundly. Through YMCA Youth Super Sports we want to help young people develop character. We want to help them learn to **care** about others, to be **honest**, to show **respect**, and to be **responsible.**

Of course, sport doesn't automatically teach these things to young people. What it does do is provide them with a good opportunity to learn about and develop these values when skillful leadership is provided by volunteer adults like you.

The YMCA Philosophy of Youth Sports

What we want youth sports to be in the YMCA is stated in our Seven Pillars of YMCA Youth Sports.

◎ **Pillar One—Everyone Plays.** We do not use tryouts to select the best players, nor do we cut kids from YMCA Youth Super Sports. Everyone who registers is assigned to a team. During the season everyone receives equal practice time and plays at least half of every game.

◎ **Pillar Two—Safety First.** Although some children may get hurt playing sports, we do all we can to prevent injuries. We've modified each sport to make it safer and more enjoyable to play. We ask you to make sure the equipment and facilities are safe and to teach the sport as we've prescribed, so that the skills taught are appropriate for children's developmental level. We ask you to develop your players' fitness levels *gradually* so they are conditioned for the sport. And we ask you to constantly supervise your young players so that you can stop any unsafe activities.

◎ **Pillar Three—Fair Play.** Fair play is about playing by the rules—and more. It's about you and your players showing respect for all who are involved in YMCA Youth Super Sports. It's about your being a role model of good sportsmanship and guiding your players to do the same. Remember, we're more interested in developing children's character through sport than in developing a few highly skilled players.

◎ **Pillar Four—Positive Competition.** We believe competition is a positive process when the pursuit of victory is kept in the right perspective. The right perspective is when adults make decisions that put the best interests of the children above winning the contest. Learning to compete is important for children, and learning to cooperate in a competitive world is an essential lesson of life. Through YMCA Youth Super Sports we want to help children learn these lessons.

◎ **Pillar Five—Family Involvement.** YMCA Youth Super Sports encourages parents to be involved appropriately along with their child's participation in our sport programs. In addition to parents being helpful as volunteer coaches, officials, and timekeepers, we encourage them to be at practices and games to support their child's participation. To help parents get involved appropriately, YMCA Youth Super Sports offers parent orientation programs.

◎ **Pillar Six—Sport for All.** YMCA Youth Super Sports is an *inclusive* sport program. That means that children who differ in various characteristics are to be included rather than excluded from participation. We offer sport programs for children who differ in physical abilities by matching them with children of similar abilities and modifying their sport. We offer programs to all children regardless of their race, gender, religious creed, or ability. We ask our adult leaders to encourage and appreciate the diversity of children in our society and to encourage the children and their parents to do the same.

◎ **Pillar Seven—Sport for Fun.** Sport is naturally fun for most children. They love the challenge of mastering the skills of the game, of playing with their friends, and of competing with their peers. Sometimes when adults become involved in children's sport, they overorganize and dominate the activity to the point of destroying children's enjoyment of the sport. If we take the fun out of sport, we are in danger of our children taking themselves out of sport. Remember that these sports are for the kids; let them have fun.

YMCA Rookies

YMCA Rookies is a skill-development program that prepares children ages 4 to 7 to participate in YMCA Winners, the *competitive* sport program, and in YMCA Champions, the personal sport-achievement program. As a coach in YMCA Rookies, we want you to focus on teaching your players the basics of the game in a precompetitive environment, where they can focus on learning the sport, not performing to win.

Too often today children are thrust into competitive sport programs with little instruction on the basics of the sport (both the skills and rules of the game). Perhaps children participate in a few practice sessions, but often they do not obtain sufficient instruction or time to develop basic skills in a precompetitive environment. Then, too, many programs do not sufficiently modify the sport to meet the physical and mental abilities of young children.

The consequence of such an introduction to sport is that children who have had early opportunities for instruction and who are physically more gifted often succeed, while those without these advantages are more likely to fail. We designed YMCA Rookies to address these problems by providing a positive introduction to sport for all children.

To ensure having the highest quality coaches, officials, and sport administrators, YMCA Youth Super Sports offers training and educational resources for all adults involved in YMCA Rookies. The purpose of this training is to emphasize the positive objectives of the program and to de-emphasize the winning-at-all-cost mentality that leads to so many negative practices in youth sport programs.

The training offered to adults involved in the program is just one aspect that makes YMCA Rookies unique. Another is the modifications we've made to the game of flag football so that children progress through the program in developmentally appropriate ways. Modifying the game increases the likelihood that children will experience success—and it reduces the risk of injury.

YMCA Winners

YMCA Winners is the values-based, competitive program in YMCA Youth Super Sports. It's for young people, ages 8 to 16, with the competition typically grouped in two- to three-year age ranges. The objectives of YMCA Winners are the same as those for YMCA Rookies: learning the skills of the game, the rules of the sport, the relationship between fitness and health, and character development. However, in YMCA Winners these objectives are achieved as players compete with other players and teams.

YMCA Champions

YMCA Champions is an innovative award program that encourages and recognizes personal sport achievement among young people ages 8 to 16. As shown in table 1.1, for young people to earn an award they must demonstrate their mastery of the sport in four areas, or domains. Within each sport they have the opportunity to earn three levels of awards.

The four content domains are the following:

1. **Knowledge.** Participants must show that they understand the rules and traditions of the sport and related fitness and health concepts.
2. **Skill.** Young people must demonstrate their mastery of the physical skills of the sport through gamelike skill tests.
3. **Participation.** Young people must participate a certain amount in practices and contests for each of the three levels.
4. **Character.** Participants must demonstrate character development through caring, honesty, respect, and responsibility.

In each sport, participants begin at the Bronze level, the first level of achievement. Once they have obtained the Bronze Award in that sport, they can move on to the Silver and Gold levels. Participants can be working on a Bronze Award in one sport, a Silver Award in another sport, and a Gold Award in a third sport. They are encouraged to progress through the levels as rapidly as they wish.

TABLE 1.1

The YMCA Champions Program

	CONTENT DOMAINS			
Levels	**Knowledge**	**Skill**	**Participation**	**Character**
Bronze				
Silver				
Gold				

Their progress is monitored by YMCA Champions coaches who act as mentors for the players. YMCA Champions coaches are assisted by Gold Leaders, players 14 years old or older who have earned the Gold Award in that sport. Gold Leaders are trained to assist younger players in their preparation for being tested in the four domains, and they assist the Champions coaches conducting the evaluations.

Once players have earned a Gold Award, they are eligible to join the YMCA Gold Club. The club is honorary and a service club, and it provides opportunities for leadership. Those who become Gold Leaders come from the membership of the YMCA Gold Club.

As a YMCA Rookies coach you will play an important role in encouraging young people to participate in both YMCA Winners and YMCA Champions. That encouragement will come not only by your urging them to participate, but also by your helping them learn the basics of the sport while having fun and building their self-worth.

chapter

2

Your Job Description

Now you know what YMCA Youth Super Sports is and what our philosophy (the Seven Pillars) is for conducting this unique sport program. You also know that YMCA Rookies emphasizes teaching children the basic skills and rules in a precompetitive environment. We'll ask you to teach your players how to play the game of flag football, but the emphasis will be on teaching and learning, not on competing in contests.

Your Duties As a Coach

Here are your seven duties as a YMCA Rookies flag football coach:

1. Teach the skills and tactics of flag football to the best of your ability. We want you to teach children the physical skills and tactics to play the sport to the best of their abilities. Kids value the learning of these skills and tactics, and they respect those who can help them master them. Be a good teacher, and remember that not all children have the same ability to learn. A few have the ability to be outstanding, many to be competent, and a few to barely play the sport. We ask that you help them all be the best that they each can be.

We'll show you an innovative games approach to teaching and practicing these skills that kids thoroughly enjoy. These games are designed to be developmentally appropriate for the children you will be teaching. You'll avoid monotonous drills, where youngsters stand in line waiting

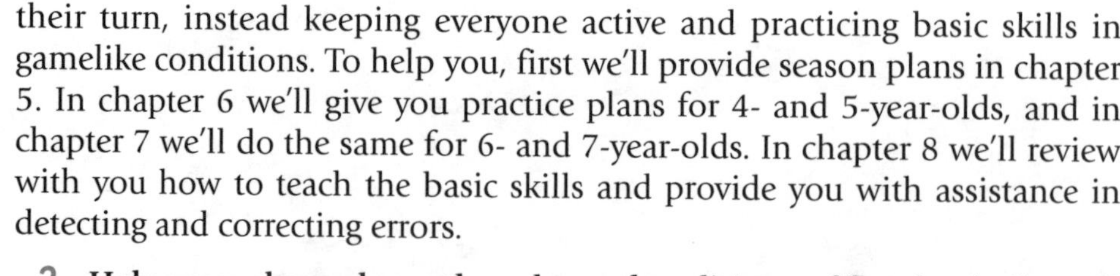

their turn, instead keeping everyone active and practicing basic skills in gamelike conditions. To help you, first we'll provide season plans in chapter 5. In chapter 6 we'll give you practice plans for 4- and 5-year-olds, and in chapter 7 we'll do the same for 6- and 7-year-olds. In chapter 8 we'll review with you how to teach the basic skills and provide you with assistance in detecting and correcting errors.

2. **Help your players learn the rules and traditions of flag football.** We'll ask you to teach your players the rules of flag football as they learn the basic skills through the modified games of the sport. Beyond the rules, we'll also ask you to teach the basic traditions of the sport. By *traditions* we mean the proper actions to take to show courtesy and avoid injury—in short, how to be a good sport. You'll find the rules and traditions in chapter 9.

3. **Help your players become fit and to value fitness for a lifetime.** We want you to help your players be fit so they can play flag football safely and successfully. But we also want more. We want you to do so in a way that your players learn to become fit on their own, understand the value of fitness, and enjoy training. Thus, we ask you not to make them do push-ups or run laps for punishment. Make it *fun to get fit* for flag football and make it fun to play flag football—so they'll stay fit for a lifetime. In chapter 10 we'll give you some tips on basic fitness for your players.

4. **Help young people develop character.** Character development is teaching children the core values: caring, honesty, respect, and responsibility. These intangible qualities are no less important to teach than passing or kicking skills. We ask you to teach these values to children by (a) conducting Team Circles, which are built into every practice plan, and (b) demonstrating and encouraging behaviors that express these values at all times. Chapter 11 will give you more suggestions about teaching character development.

5. **Ensure the safety of your players.** You are responsible for supervising every aspect of your players' participation in flag football. Make sure the field is clear of hazardous objects and that the kids do not engage in activities that might injure themselves or others. You have not only a legal but also a moral responsibility to supervise them closely. See chapter 10 for more on safety.

6. **Help each child develop a positive sense of self-worth.** An essential goal in conducting YMCA Youth Super Sports programs is to help children gain a strong, positive sense of their worth as human beings. For each of us, our most important possession is our self-worth. Please teach our children flag football in a way that helps them grow to respect themselves and others.

7. **Make it fun.** Make learning the game a fantastic, positive experience so that your players will want to continue playing for many years to come.

Being a Good Coach

Just what makes a good flag football coach?

A person who knows the sport of flag football well. If you're not that familiar with the sport, be sure to attend the YMCA Rookies Flag Football Coaches Course and study more about the sport. Refer to the list of videos in appendix A.

A person who wants to teach flag football to young people, who cares. Excellent teachers are motivated, have a positive attitude, and give the time to do the job well.

A person who understands young people, who possesses empathy. Empathy is caring about the young people you teach by showing you understand them.

We hope you'll do your best to be a good flag football coach for the children on your team. By doing so, you can help them develop their spirits, minds, and bodies—the goal for all YMCA programs.

chapter

3

Remember They're Kids

One of the challenges of working with youngsters is to relate to them *as children*, not as miniature adults. To do this, you need to understand "where they're coming from"—that is, where they are in their development physically, socially, emotionally, and intellectually. What makes it especially interesting is that on any team you coach, you're likely to find both early maturers and late bloomers. Furthermore, this variance applies not only to your group as a whole, but to each individual within it. That is, one child may be quite intellectually mature and quick to understand flag football tactics and skills, but he may be slow in physical development and thus have difficulty in successfully executing the skills. Another may be very developed physically but underdeveloped emotionally.

The more familiar you are with the physical capabilities and mind-sets of the children, the better you'll be able to communicate with youngsters and help them grow through their experiences in flag football. The following lists detail children's development physically, socially, emotionally, and cognitively. Realize that each child will not conform to all the characteristics on these lists at any given age; this doesn't mean the child is abnormal. The information here provides a general understanding of children's developmental characteristics. While we can't take you back to when you were 4 to 7 years of age, we can help you remember what it was like—and help you better understand and relate to children.

4- and 5-Year-Olds

Physical Characteristics

At 4

- Children's running, jumping, hopping, throwing, and catching become better coordinated.
- Galloping and one-foot skipping begin to appear.
- They can ride a tricycle.

At 5

- Children are 3 1/2 to 3 3/4 feet tall. They may grow from 2 to 3 inches and gain from 3 to 6 pounds during the year.
- Girls may be about a year ahead of boys in physiological development.
- Children are beginning to have better body control.
- Their large muscles are better developed than the small muscles that control the fingers and hands.
- Their eye and hand coordination is not yet complete.
- Children are vigorous and noisy, but their activity appears to have a definite direction.
- They tire easily and need plenty of rest.

Social Characteristics

At 4

- Children form their first friendships.
- They are becoming less likely to play alone and more likely to play interactively with others.

At 5

- Children are interested in neighborhood games with other children. They sometimes play games to test their skill.
- They like being with other children, and they seem to get along best in small groups.

Development characteristics are adapted from the following:

From Berk, Laura E., *Development Through the Lifespan.* Copyright © 1998 by Allyn & Bacon. Adapted by permission.

From Humphrey, James H., *Sports for Children: A Guide for Adults.* Copyright © 1993 by Charles C Thomas, Publisher, Ltd. Adapted by permission.

- Their interests are largely self-centered.
- Children imitate when they play.
- They get along well in taking turns, and they respect others' belongings.
- Children show an interest in home activities.

Emotional Characteristics

At 4

- Self-conscious emotions (shame, embarrassment, guilt, envy, and pride) become more common.

At 5

- Children seldom show jealousy toward younger siblings.
- Children usually see only one way to do things and one answer to a question.
- They are inclined not to change plans in the middle of an activity; instead, they'd rather start over.
- They may fear being deprived of their mothers.
- They are learning to get along better, but they still may resort to quarreling and fighting.
- They like to be trusted with errands and enjoy performing simple tasks. They want to please and to do what is expected of them.
- They can better interpret, predict, and influence others' emotional reactions.
- They are beginning to sense right and wrong in terms of specific situations.

Cognitive Characteristics

At 4

- They can generalize remembered information from one situation to another.
- They have a basic understanding of causality in familiar situations.

At 5

- They enjoy copying designs, letters, and numbers, and they like counting objects.
- They are interested in completing tasks.
- Their memory for past events is good.
- They are able to plan activities.
- These children may tend to monopolize table conversation.

- They look at books and pretend to read.
- They like recordings, music, and words that tell stories. They also enjoy stories, dramatic plays, and poems.
- Children of this age can sing simple melodies, beat accurate rhythms, and recognize simple tunes. They enjoy making up dances to music.
- Their daydreams seem to center around make-believe play.
- They have more than 2,000 words in their speaking vocabularies, and their pronunciation is usually clear. They can speak in complete sentences and can express their needs well in words.
- Their attention span may have increased up to 20 minutes in some cases.

6- and 7-Year-Olds

Physical Characteristics

At 6

- Children are 3 1/2 to 4 feet tall and grow gradually.
- They usually have a lot of energy.
- They like to move, doing such things as running, jumping, and chasing. They enjoy dodging games.
- Their muscular control is becoming more effective with large objects.
- A noticeable change occurs in eye-hand coordination. Children can tie their shoes and write their names.
- Children's legs are lengthening rapidly.

At 7

- They may grow 2 to 3 inches and gain 3 to 5 pounds during the year.
- They may tire easily and show fatigue in the afternoon.
- Whole-body movements are under better control.
- Children can throw better and catch more accurately.
- Children's reaction times are slow.
- Eye-hand coordination improves still more.
- Children's hearts and lungs are smallest in proportion to their body size.
- Children may be susceptible to disease and have low resistance.
- Children's endurance is low.
- Small accessory muscles are developing.

Social Characteristics

At 6

- These children are self-centered and need praise.
- They like to be first.
- Sex differences are not of great importance to them at this age.
- They enjoy group play when groups are small.
- Children like parties, but their behavior may not always be proper.
- Most of them like school and have a desire to learn.
- They are interested in the conduct of their friends.
- They show an interest in group approval.

At 7

- They want recognition for individual achievements.
- They are not always good losers.
- They often talk about their families.
- They are interested in friends and not concerned with their friends' social or economic status.
- They begin to learn to stand up for their own rights.
- Some children may have nervous habits, such as nail biting, tongue sucking, scratching, or pulling on the ear.
- Children are beginning to have a sense of time.
- Children show signs of being more cooperative.

Emotional Characteristics

At 6

- Anger may be difficult to control at times.
- Behavior may often be explosive and unpredictable.
- Sometimes children show jealousy toward siblings, but at other times the children take pride in them.
- They are greatly excited by anything new.
- They may be self-assertive and dramatic.

At 7

- Children have more control over anger.
- They become less impulsive and boisterous than at 6 years.

- Their curiosity and creative desires may condition their responses.
- Children are critical of themselves and sensitive to failure. It may be difficult for them to take criticism from adults, and they are overanxious to reach the goals set for them by parents and teachers.
- Children want to be more independent. They reach for new experiences and try to relate to a larger world.

Cognitive Characteristics

At 6

- They have a speaking vocabulary of more than 2,500 words.
- Their interest span is likely to be short.
- They know number combinations up to 10 and the comparative values of common coins.
- They can define objects in terms of what they are used for.
- They know the right and left sides of the body.
- Their drawings are crude but realistic.
- They can contribute to guided group planning.
- Their conversations usually are concerned with their own experiences and interests.
- Children at this age have a lively curiosity, and their memory is strong.
- They identify with imaginary characters.

At 7

- Their attention span is still short, but they do not object to repetition. They can listen longer at 7 years of age than they could at age 6.
- Their reaction time is still slow.
- They are becoming more realistic and less imaginative.
- They can read some books themselves.
- They can reason, but they have little experience on which to base their judgments.
- They can barely begin to think abstractly.
- They are learning to evaluate the achievements of themselves and others.
- They are concerned with their own lack of skill and achievement.

chapter

4

The Games Approach to Teaching Flag Football

Do you remember from when you were a kid how adults taught you to play a sport, either in an organized sport program or a physical education class? They probably taught you the basic skills using a series of drills that, if the truth be known, you found boring. As you began to learn the basic skills, they eventually taught you the tactics of the game, showing you when to use these skills in various game situations. Do you remember how impatient you became during what seemed to be endless instruction—and how much you just wanted to play?

Can you recall when you learned a sport by playing with a group of your friends in the neighborhood? You didn't learn the basic skills first; you had no time for that. You began playing immediately. If you didn't know the basic things to do, your friends told you quickly during the game so they could keep playing. Try to remember an experience like that, because we're going to ask you to use a very similar approach, called the "games approach," to teaching flag football to young people, an approach we think knocks the socks off the traditional approach.

On the surface, it would seem to make sense to teach flag football by first teaching the basic skills of the sport and then the tactics of the game. Well, forget this traditional approach to teaching sports! We've discovered that this traditional approach has two serious shortcomings. First, it teaches the skills of the sport out of the context of the game. Kids learn to run pass patterns and catch the ball, but they find it difficult to learn how to use these skills within the game. That is, they don't understand the tactics of the game.

Second, learning skills by doing drills outside of the context of the game is so-o-o-o boring. The single biggest turnoff about how adults teach kids sport is that we overorganize the instruction and deprive kids of their intrinsic desire to play the game.

We're asking that as a YMCA Rookies coach you teach flag football the YMCA way instead, the games approach way. Clear the old, traditional approach out of your mind. Once you fully understand the games approach, you'll quickly see its superiority in teaching flag football. Not only will kids learn the game better, but you and they will also have much more fun. And, as a bonus, you'll have far fewer discipline problems.

With the games approach, all teaching of skills begins by playing the game, usually a version of the game modified for younger children. As the children play the game, you help them learn "what to do," what we call *tactical awareness*. When your players understand what they must do in the game, they are then eager to develop the skills to play the game. Once your players are motivated to learn the skills, you can demonstrate the skills of the game, have youngsters practice using gamelike drills, and provide individual instruction by identifying players' errors and helping to correct them.

In the traditional approach to teaching sports, players do this:

Learn the skill → Learn the tactics → Play the game

In the games approach, players do this:

Play the game → Learn the tactics → Learn the skill

In the past, adults have often placed too much emphasis on learning the skills and not enough on learning how to play skillfully—that is, how to use those skills during play. The games approach, in contrast, emphasizes learning what to do first, then how to do it. Moreover—and this is important—the games approach lets kids discover what to do in the game not by your telling them, but by *their experiencing* it. What you do as an effective coach is help them discover what they've already experienced.

In contrast to the "skill-drill-kill the enthusiasm" approach, the games approach is a guided discovery method of teaching. It empowers your kids to solve the problems that arise in the game, and that's a big part of the fun in learning a game.

Now let's look more closely at the games approach to see the four-step process for teaching flag football:

1. Play a modified game.
2. Help the players discover what they need to do to play the game successfully.
3. Teach the skills of the game.
4. Practice the skills in another game.

Step 1. Play a Modified Game

OK, it's the first day of practice; some of the kids are eager to get started, others are obviously apprehensive. Some have rarely thrown a football, most don't know the rules, and none know the positions. What do you do?

If you teach using the traditional approach, you start with a little warm-up activity, then line the players up for a simple hitting drill and go from there. If you teach using the games approach, you begin by playing a modified game that is developmentally appropriate for the level of the players and also designed to focus on learning a specific part of the game.

Don't worry about modifying the game to be developmentally appropriate—we've done that for you. Our practice plans in part II are based mainly on six-player teams. We've also modified the size of the field, the ball, and the rules. We'll tell you more about these changes later.

The second reason to modify the game is to emphasize only a limited number of situations in the game. This is one way you guide your players to discover certain tactics in the game.

For instance, you have your players play a 3 v 3 (three players versus three players) game, making the objective of the game for receivers to run routes and get open to receive passes. Playing the game this way forces players to think about what they have to do to accomplish this.

Step 2. Help the Players Discover What They Need to Do

As your players are playing the game, look for the right spot to "freeze" the action, step in, and hold a brief question-and-answer session to discuss problems they were having in carrying out the goal of the game. You don't need to pop in on the first miscue, but if they repeat the same types of mental or physical mistakes a few times in a row, step in and ask them questions that relate to the goal of the game and the necessary skills required. The best time to interrupt the game is when you notice that they are having trouble carrying out the main goal, or aim, of the game. By stopping the game, freezing action, and asking questions, you'll help them understand

- what the aim of the game is;
- what they must do to achieve that aim; and
- what skills they must use to achieve that aim.

After you've discussed the aim, you can begin the skill practice.

Here's an example of how to use questions in the games approach, continuing the example of the modified game we used earlier. Your players just played a game in which the objective was for receivers to run routes and get open to receive passes. You see that they are having trouble doing this, so you interrupt the action and ask the following questions:

Coach: What were the receivers trying to do?
Players: Get open to catch passes.

Coach: How do you get open?
Players: By running to where the defender isn't, and running different routes.

Coach: That's right. Let's learn one of those routes—the square out.

Through the modified game and skillful questioning on your part, your players realize that running specific routes is essential to their success. Just as important, rather than telling them that this skill is critical, you led them to that discovery through a well-designed modified game and through questions. This questioning that leads to players' discovery is a crucial part of the games approach. Essentially you'll be asking your players—usually literally—"What do you need to do to succeed in this situation?"

Asking the right questions is a very important part of your teaching. We've given you sample questions in each practice plan (see chapters 6 and 7) to help you know where to begin. At first, asking questions will be difficult because your players have so little experience with the game. If you've learned sports through the traditional approach, you'll be tempted to tell your players how to play the game and not waste time asking them questions. Resist this powerful temptation to tell them what to do, and especially don't tell them before they begin to play the game.

If your players have trouble understanding what to do, phrase your questions to let them choose between one option and another. For example, if you ask them, "What's the best way to catch a high pass?" and get answers such as, "With your hands," or "With your arms stretched out," then ask, "Do you catch it with your little fingers or your thumbs together?"

Sometimes players need to have more time playing the game, or you may need to make a further modification to the game so that it is even easier for them to discover what they are to do. This discovery method takes more patience on your part, but it's a powerful way to learn. Don't be reluctant to change the numbers in the teams or some aspect of the structure of the game to aid this discovery.

Step 3. Teach the Skills of the Game

Only after your players have recognized—from actually playing the game—what skills they need do you want to use focused drills to teach them the specific skills. Now you can use a more traditional approach to teaching sports skills, nicknamed IDEA:

I Introduce the skill.
D Demonstrate the skill.
E Explain the skill.
A Attend to players practicing the skill.

Let's take a closer look at each part of the approach.

Introduce the Skill

Your players will already have some idea of what the skill is that you want to teach because they've already tried it during a game and talked about it. This is an opportunity to get them focused on the specific skill. You can do this in three ways:

◎ **First get their attention.** Make sure your players are positioned where they all can see and hear you—ask them if they can before you begin the training. Be sure they are not facing a bright light or some other distraction. When you speak, be enthusiastic, talk slightly louder than normal, and look your players in the eye.

◎ **Next name the skill.** If the skill is referred to by more than one name, choose one and stick with it. This helps prevent confusion and makes it easier for you and your players to communicate.

◎ **Finally briefly review how the skill will help them in the game.** They should have some idea from your earlier questioning, but make sure they see how it fits in the game and describe how the skill relates to more advanced skills.

Demonstrate the Skill

Players, especially younger ones, can learn a lot more from seeing the skill performed than from just hearing about it. It's important that the skill be shown correctly, so if you don't feel you can demonstrate it well, have another adult or a skilled player do it. Here are some tips for demonstrating a skill:

- ◎ Use correct form.
- ◎ Demonstrate the skill several times.
- ◎ During one or two performances, slow down the action so players can see every movement involved in the skill.
- ◎ Perform the skill at different angles so your players can get a full perspective on it.
- ◎ Demonstrate the skill from both the right and left sides.

Explain the Skill

Help your players understand what they see in the demonstration by giving them a short and simple explanation. Relate the skill to previously learned skills whenever possible.

To see if your explanation is working, ask your players whether they understand it. A good way to do this is to have them repeat the explanation back to you. Ask questions ("What are you going to do first?" "Then what?") and watch for players who look confused or uncertain. Try to explain the skill using different words, which may give the youngsters a different perspective.

Since you are working with young children, who have short attention spans, try to take no more than three minutes to do the introduction, demonstration, and explanation. Follow it *immediately* with practice.

Attend to Players Practicing the Skill

The practice plans found in chapters 6 and 7 will provide you with specific ideas on how to run the practice, as well as cue words you should use during practice. Use these cues to help children remember what to focus on during practice.

As your players practice, watch them closely to see which ones can use additional help. Some children will need you to physically guide them through the skill; doing this will help them gain the confidence they need to try. Most will just need some feedback from you, and they'll be glad to get it—if you do it the right way.

Nobody likes to be yelled at, especially when they're supposed to be having fun! The young children you are working with have little or no prior experience with flag football, or even sports in general. They also have not fully developed their motor skills, so you should expect to see more incorrect than correct movements during practice. If you lose your cool when a player makes a mistake, you're just teaching that player to stop trying or to get upset about errors—not exactly what you had in mind. Let your players know that making mistakes isn't the end of the world.

If you have to correct a player, be sure not to follow a positive statement with the word *but.* For example, don't say, "Jordan, your grip on the ball is great, but you need to follow through on your passes." Saying it this way causes many kids to ignore the positive statement and focus on the negative one. Instead of the word *but,* use the word *and.* Say something like "Jordan, your grip on the ball is great, and now let's work on your follow through."

Praise from you is very motivational for your players. Be sure to tell them what they are *doing right* as well as help them correct what they are doing wrong.

Also emphasize positive rather than negative errors. For example, a defender in a zone defense may play the ball well but drift out of his or her zone. This is better than staying in your zone but not covering receivers well.

Step 4. Practice the Skills in Another Game

Once the players have practiced the skill, you then put them in a second game situation. This will give them the chance to integrate the skill they've learned into actual game play. After having practiced the skill, they should be more successful in comparison with their performance in the first game.

So, that's the games approach. Your players will get to play more in practice, and once they learn how the skills fit in with their performance and enjoyment of the game, they'll be more motivated to work on those skills, which will help them to be successful.

Part II

The Coaching Plans

Now you understand what your job is as a coach, especially the games approach to teaching flag football that we want you to use. In this part we'll map out what we want you to teach players. In chapter 5 we'll present the season plans for what you'll teach the entire season, not only the skills and tactics, but also the rules and traditions, the health and fitness concepts, and a few key character development concepts. Then in chapter 6 we provide you with 10 practice plans for 4- to 5-year-olds, and in chapter 7 we provide 10 practice plans for 6- to 7-year-olds. When you want to know more about how to teach a skill, a rule, or a fitness or character concept listed in the practice plans, you'll find it in part III.

chapter

5

The Season Plans

If you're feeling a bit overwhelmed by the job you've taken on, here's where we give you specific guidance on what to teach. This chapter provides an overview of the season plans for each of the two age groups; it will be followed by separate chapters of practice plans for each group.

The season plans we've laid out have five components:

- Purpose
- Tactics and skills
- Rules and traditions
- Fitness concepts
- Character development concepts

Here's a brief description of each component:

- **Purpose.** This is the overall purpose of the particular practice—what you are focusing on for that practice.

- **Tactics and skills.** These are the main tactics and skills you will be focusing on during the practice—for example, passing, or running square-out and curl pass patterns. They are not the *only* tactics and skills that will come into play during the practice; they are simply your main focus for that day.

- **Rules and traditions.** These are the rules that kids need to know. The rules and traditions are taught gradually, as part of playing games and learning skills. Traditions are those unwritten rules that players follow to be courteous and safe, such as shaking hands with opponents at the end of a game.

◎ **Health and fitness concepts.** Even young children can understand some simple health and fitness concepts, such as the idea that exercise strengthens the heart. Some of these concepts should be the focus for brief discussions during practice, and they are built into each practice in Fitness Circles.

◎ **Character development concepts.** The four YMCA core values—caring, honesty, respect, and responsibility—can all be related to many situations that arise while playing flag football. For example, playing cooperatively with teammates shows that you care about them. We'll suggest some specific ideas for briefly discussing character development values in Team Circles at the end of practice.

Season Plan for 4- to 5-Year-Olds

At these ages, children need understanding and skills to enable them to play a game. Tactically, this means helping them to see the need to play good pass defense and play as a team, as well as learning individual skills. We give an overview on the next page that you can use as a weekly guide. It reflects the tactics and skills, rules and traditions, and fitness and character development concepts that you should cover. All of these will be described in more detail in the practice plans in chapter 6.

4- to 5-Year-Olds

Week	Purpose	Tactics and skills	Rules and traditions	Fitness concepts	Character development concepts
1	To learn basic offensive skills	Passing, catching	Passing rules	**General fitness** Learn heart size and location.	**Four core values** Incorporate the four core values.
2	To learn basic offensive skills	Passing, catching	Receiving rules	**General fitness** Heart pumps blood through blood vessels.	**Responsibility** Stay under control.
3	To learn a pass pattern	Square-outs	No-block rule	**General fitness** Learn lung size and location.	**Responsibility** Work together as a team.
4	To set up the offensive attack	Passing, catching, curls, running pass patterns	Defensive rules	**Cardiorespiratory fitness** Exercise increases heart and lung strength.	**Honesty** Be honest if you make a mistake.
5	To stop offensive progress	Pulling flags	Flag guarding	**Muscle fitness** Exercise increases muscle strength.	**Respect** Respect all players in the game.
6	To learn a new pass pattern	Slants	Running rules	**Muscle fitness** Flexibility is how far a muscle can stretch or a joint can move.	**Caring** Care enough to share the ball.
7	To run effective pass patterns and get open	Passing, catching, running pass patterns	Offsides	**Training and conditioning** Warming up helps prevent injuries and gets your body ready to play flag football.	**Caring** Be supportive of your teammates.
8	To learn a new pass pattern	Streaks	Pass interference	**Safety** Learn to define personal space.	**Responsibility** Everyone has a role to play.
9	To run effective pass patterns and get open	Passing, catching, running pass patterns	Illegal rushing	**Healthy habits** Exercise requires fluid replacement.	**Responsibility** You are responsible to everyone on the team.
10	To cover pass receivers	Covering receivers	Defensive holding	**Healthy habits** Snacks are any foods you eat between meals.	**Keeping perspective** Learn and have fun while playing.

Season Plan for 6- to 7-Year-Olds

These slightly older players will not only revisit the tactics and skills they have learned earlier, they will also add new tactics and skills—such as new pass routes—along the way. The overview on the next page provides a weekly guide as described previously. The tactics and skills, rules and traditions, and fitness and character development concepts all will be detailed in the practice plans in chapter 7.

6- to 7-Year-Olds

Week	Purpose	Tactics and skills	Rules and traditions	Fitness concepts	Character development concepts
1	To learn basic offensive skills	Passing, catching	Passing rules	**General fitness** Hearts work without any rest.	**Four core values** Incorporate the four core values.
2	To learn basic offensive skills	Passing, catching	Receiving rules	**General fitness** Learn about lung function.	**Responsibility** Be responsible to your teammates.
3	To learn a pass pattern	Square-outs, carrying ball after a catch	No-block rule	**Cardiorespiratory health and fitness** Learn about cardiorespiratory exercises.	**Responsibility** Be a good sport.
4	To learn two new pass patterns	Curl, slant	Defensive rules	**Muscle fitness** Muscles need to be exercised every other day to get stronger.	**Honesty** Be honest if you make a mistake.
5	To stop offensive progressive	Pulling flags	Flag guarding	**Muscle fitness** Good flexibility helps prevent injuries.	**Responsibility** Stay under control.
6	To learn a new pass pattern	Streaks	Running rules	**Body type** There are three basic body types.	**Responsibility** Don't make excuses about mistakes.
7	To run effective pass patterns and get open	Passing, catching, running pass patterns	Offsides	**Training and conditioning** Warm up for 5 to 10 minutes before playing.	**Caring** Share the ball with your teammates.
8	To learn a new pass pattern	Post pattern	Illegal rushing	**Training and conditioning** The cool-down returns heart rate to a normal level.	**Respect** Respect your teammates.
9	To run effective pass patterns and get open	Various routes	Defensive holding	**Healthy habits** Water is great for replacing liquids lost during practice.	**Caring** Be supportive of your teammates.
10	To cover pass receivers	Covering receivers	Pass interference	**Healthy habits** Smoking causes many diseases.	**Respect** Respect the sport.

chapter

6

Practice Plans for 4- to 5-Year-Olds

This chapter contains 10 practice plans to use with your 4- and 5-year-old YMCA Rookies flag football players. Before we get to those plans though, we'll explain the modifications to the game that are used in Rookies play, and we'll give you a quick overview of what's in the practice plans and how they are to be used.

Game Modifications

YMCA Rookies play 6 v 6 games. This speeds up the game and gives all the kids more opportunities to be involved in play. Have no more than 12 players on a team.

The field is also smaller than regulation; we recommend a 30-yard by 60-yard field. Again, to keep kids active and to give them more touches of the ball and opportunities to learn, you will see that we quite often recommend having two 3 v 3 games going at once, on separate halves of the field, or three-player teams performing games and skill practices in separate quadrants of the field. We highly recommend you have at least one assistant coach to help you watch and instruct the players. Encourage parents to help you; the more assistants you have, the more attention each child can get.

Another modification is in the ball itself: we recommend using either a Nerf ball or a youth-size ball (10 1/4 to 10 1/2 inches). If you do try the youth-size ball and find that your players are having trouble gripping or throwing it, be ready to switch to the Nerf ball.

Many of the rules for flag football have been adapted to make them more appropriate for the age and skill level of 4- and 5-year-olds. For example, at this level blocking is not allowed, kickoffs and punting do not take place, there are no running plays, and all offensive players are eligible to receive forward passes. See chapter 9 for more on flag football rules.

Practice Plan Organization

Each plan contains the following sections:

- Purpose
- Equipment
- Warm-Up
- Fitness Circle
- Game 1
- Skill Practice(s)
- Game 2
- Team Circle

Purpose focuses on what you want to teach your players during that practice; it is your main theme for that day. *Equipment* notes what you'll need on hand for that practice (and the size of the field). The *Warm-Up* section gives you 5 to 10 minutes of warm-up activities. This segment will be followed by 5 minutes of the *Fitness Circle*, during which you briefly talk with players about an idea that relates to health or fitness. Then, in *Game 1*, you'll play a game that puts your players in a game-like situation and introduces them to the main tactic or skill that you want them to learn that day. (Note that in some games we say, play a "hot" defense or a "cold" defense. A "hot" defense is one that is going all-out, trying its hardest to stop the offense. A "cold" defense is one that is playing at about half speed, in more of a "contain" situation—perhaps putting light pressure on the quarterback but not trying to down him or her, or playing a bit off the receivers, allowing them to make catches and then closing in on them.)

Then, using the games approach as described in chapter 4, you'll guide your players through a short question-and-answer session that leads to the *Skill Practice*. (We've provided sample responses for your players so you can see where to guide them.) Here you will have one or two skill practices in which you will teach players the skill and then conduct a fun drill for them to practice that skill. Remember to use the IDEA approach to teaching skills, as described in chapter 4.

Chapter 8 contains descriptions of all the skills, so a page reference will be given to guide you to the appropriate description there. The introduction, demonstration, and explanation should be very brief to fit young children's short attention spans. As the players practice, you attend to individual children, guiding them with *Coach's Cues* (which are provided in the practice plans) or further demonstration.

After the skill practices, you will go on to *Game 2*. Have the kids play another game to let them use the skills they just learned and to see how those skills fit into the context of a game. We provide *Coach's Points* for you to help your players focus on the most important points. And with many practices, we provide *Variations* to give you ideas on how to modify the games to make them easier or more challenging, based on your observations of your players' skill levels.

The practice concludes with a *Team Circle*, which focuses on character development. You take about 5 minutes to talk *with* (not just *to*) your players about some aspect of the game that relates to one of the four core values—caring, honesty, respect, and responsibility. Following this, you wrap up the practice with a reminder of the next practice day and time and a preview of what will be taught in that next practice.

A note about Fitness and Team Circles—these times are meant to be true discussions, not lectures where you do all the talking and the kids do all the listening. Ask the questions provided and wait for your players to respond. Don't feed them the answers that we provide; these answers are only meant to help you guide the discussion. The kids' wording of answers doesn't have to match what we give here; that wording is presented for your benefit so that you know where to guide the players. Your role in Team Circles is as much to ask questions and get players to respond as it is to dole out information.

The plans in this chapter, combined with the information in the rest of this book, should give you everything you need to lead practices. Just remember to be patient and caring as you work on skills. Kids will progress at different rates, and it's more important that they learn the sport in a positive way than it is for them to learn quickly.

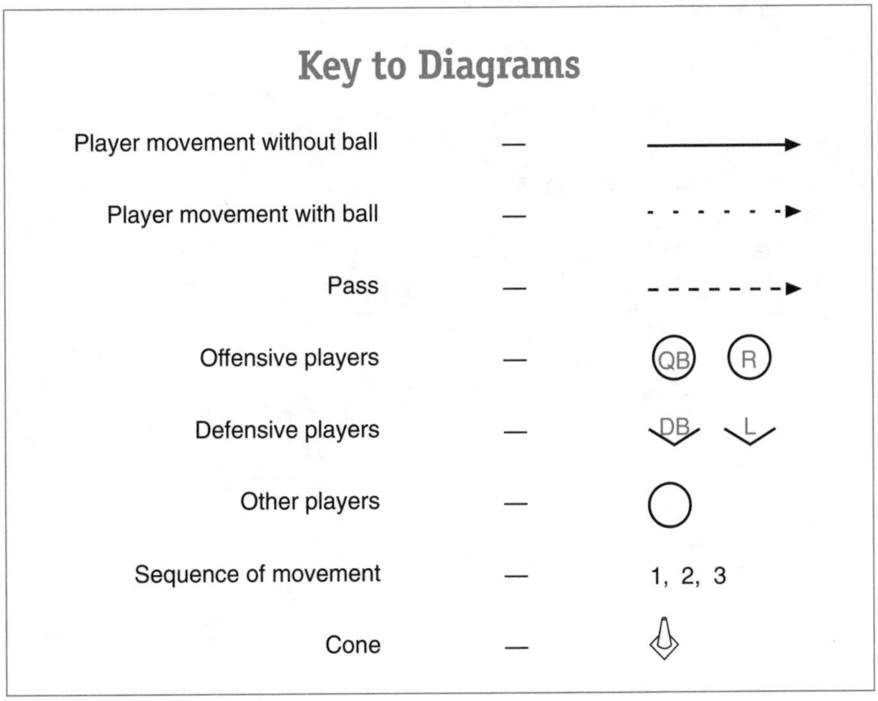

Key to Diagrams

Player movement without ball	—	———→
Player movement with ball	—	· · · · · · →
Pass	—	- - - - - - - →
Offensive players	—	QB R
Defensive players	—	DB L
Other players	—	○
Sequence of movement	—	1, 2, 3
Cone	—	

Practice 1

PURPOSE

To learn basic offensive skills

Equipment

- One football for every two players (Nerf ball or youth-size: 10 1/4- to 10 1/2-inch)
- Grass field 30 yards by 60 yards

Warm-Up (10 minutes)

Begin each practice with 5 to 10 minutes of warm-up activities to get players loosened up and ready to go.

Have the kids jog one lap around the field and get into a circle. Lead them in five jumping jacks and stretches for their legs and arms.

Fitness Circle (5 minutes)

Following the warm-up, gather the players and briefly discuss the fitness concept for that practice.

Key Idea: General fitness

Gather the children into a group. "Make a fist. That's *how big* your heart is. Place your fist on your chest. That is *where* your heart is. You can't see it, but it's there. While everyone's heart is at the same spot, everyone has a different heart size. A person's heart is as big as their fist. So that means that some hearts are big and some are small. Think of your dad's, uncle's, or older brother's fist. His heart is (or their hearts are) a lot bigger than yours. What about the heart of a big football player?"

Activity: Heart rhyme

Have the children sing the following to the tune of "Mulberry Bush."

Your body has a heart, heart, heart,
heart, heart, heart,
heart, heart, heart,
Your body has a heart, heart, heart,
Point to where it is.
Your body has a heart, heart, heart,
heart, heart, heart,
heart, heart, heart,
Your body has a heart, heart, heart,
And it's the size of your FIST. (Shout the last word.)

Practice 1

Game 1 (10 minutes)

Following the Fitness Circle, get the kids playing a game. Then interrupt each game with a time of questions and answers—with you asking the questions and your players providing the answers (about what the goal of the game was and what skills and tactics they needed to perform to succeed in the game). For many games, we provide diagrams or figures showing how the game is played. We also often provide coaching points for you to pass along to your players during the games.

Goal

Players will get the ball into the end zone.

Description

Play two simultaneous 3 v 3 games. On defense, play player-to-player. The offense starts at midfield and moves downfield in a nonstop passing game—no huddles, no plays, just receivers moving downfield and catching the ball. They are down where they catch it—and the receiver who caught the ball becomes the quarterback, as his or her two teammates immediately go out for passes farther down the field. The defense becomes the offense on an interception or incomplete pass—otherwise the offense keeps moving down the field until they score, so long as they keep completing passes. (You may want to allow the offense to have three incomplete passes before the ball changes hands; keep the game moving, but don't make it too confusing for the players.) Give one point for each completed pass and six points for each touchdown.

Coach: What's the goal of this game?
Players: To get the ball into the end zone.

Coach: How do you do that?
Players: By throwing the ball so my teammates can catch it.

Coach: How do you throw the ball?
Players: Use the right grip and arm motion.

You'll follow game 1 with one or more skill practices, during which you'll introduce, demonstrate, and explain a skill or tactic, and then attend to your players as they practice it. The question-and-answer session, in which your players tell you what skills and tactics they needed to be successful in the game, leads directly to the skill practice. Remember, the sample player responses are your cue as to where to guide them. We often provide coaching points with the skill practices; pass these points along to your players. We also provide Coach's Cues—phrases to help your players focus on the task at hand—in many skill practices and games.

Skill Practice (15 minutes)

1. Introduce, demonstrate, and explain how to *throw the football* (see page 120).
2. Have players practice throwing.

Description

Players in pairs play catch, standing about 3 yards apart. Have them hold the ball high for good rotation and release.

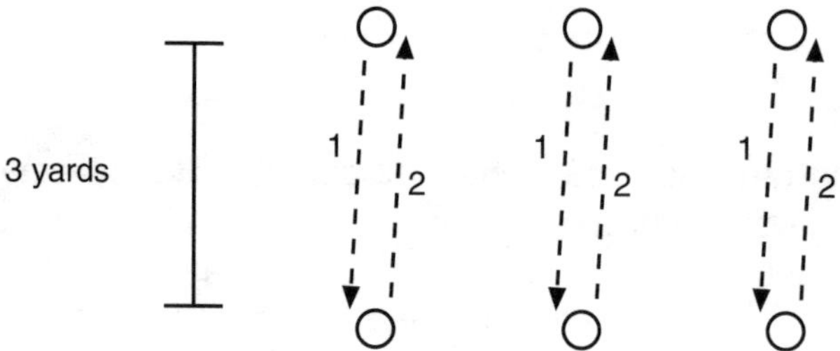

"Spread your fingers on the ball."
"Hold the ball behind your ear."
"Snap your wrist!"

Game 2 (15 minutes)

Goal

Players will move the ball downfield and score.

Description

Repeat game 1.

☞ Learning the basic throwing motion is important for success in flag football and many other sports.

☞ Go over passing rules (see page 131).

Practice 1

Team Circle (5 minutes)

Conclude practice by gathering your players and discussing a character development concept. These aren't lectures; you want your players' active participation in these discussions. Following the discussions, wrap up the practice with a few comments.

Key Idea: Four core values

Gather the children into a circle. "This season we'll talk about four qualities of a good person and teammate. Number one is caring. Can you tell me ways you show caring to others? Helping someone up when they fall? Good! Number two is honesty. What ways do you show honesty? How about if you tell someone if you broke something? That's honesty. Number three is respect. Do you know what respect is? One thing that shows respect is listening to adults when they speak to you, like you're doing now. Number four is responsibility. One way to show you're responsible is to clean up after yourself. Don't wait for others to clean up for you." Ask them to share ways they show the four values in other areas of their lives. "Good teammates show these values to each other. We'll talk more about these four values during the season."

Wrap-Up

Make summary comments about practice. Remind players of the next practice day and time.

Practice 2

☞ **PURPOSE**

To learn basic offensive skills

Equipment

- ☑ One football for every two players (Nerf ball or youth-size: 10 1/4- to 10 1/2-inch)
- ☑ Grass field 30 yards by 60 yards

Warm-Up (10 minutes)

Have the players jog one lap around the field and then come back and get into a circle. Lead them in five jumping jacks and stretches for their legs and arms.

Fitness Circle (5 minutes)

Key Idea: General fitness

Equipment: Bicycle pump (optional)

Gather the children into a group. "Your heart has the job of pushing blood all around your body. To do that, it must pump the blood through tubes called blood vessels." (The children may call these tubes veins, although technically they are arteries and veins.) "What is a pump?" (You may get blank stares.) "Can you give me an example of a pump?" [Gasoline pump, bicycle pump, basketball/football pump.] "What do pumps pump?" [Air, gasoline, or blood!]

If you have a bicycle pump, demonstrate how it works to the children. Explain that instead of pumping air, your heart pumps blood.

Activity: Heart pump

Have the children jump up and down as they say this rhyme:

Jump, jump hearts pump
Pump, pump all jump
All jump pump, pump
Hearts pump jump, jump.

"Have you ever felt your heart pumping?" (Some may say that after running they feel their hearts beating in their heads or see their chests moving.)

Game 1 (10 minutes)

Goal

Players will move the ball downfield and score.

Description

Play two simultaneous 3 v 3 games. On defense, play player-to-player. The offense starts at midfield and moves downfield in a nonstop passing game—no huddles, no plays, just receivers moving downfield and catching the ball. They are down where they catch it—and the receiver

Practice 2

who caught the ball becomes the quarterback, as his or her two teammates immediately go out for passes farther down the field. The defense becomes the offense on an interception or incomplete pass—otherwise the offense keeps moving down the field until they score, so long as they keep completing passes. (You may want to allow the offense to have three incomplete passes before the ball changes hands; keep the game moving, but don't make it too confusing for the players.) Give one point for each completed pass and six points for each touchdown.

Coach: What were you trying to do?
Players: Complete passes and move downfield to score.

Coach: How do we keep the ball moving downfield?
Player: By making good passes and good catches.

Skill Practice 1 (10 minutes)

Put players in groups of two and have them play catch 3 to 5 yards apart. Increase the distance as they increase their skill. Make sure they have a good release and hold the ball high. (See the diagram on page 120.)

"Hold the ball tight!"
"Keep your weight on the back foot."
"Follow through with your arm across your body."

Skill Practice 2 (10 minutes)

Divide players into groups of twos. Give each pair a football. Instruct them to throw 10 balls from a sitting position to each other. This drill is used for developing arm strength, wrist snap, and accuracy. Start out at 3 yards apart and work up to 5 yards apart.

Game 2 (10 minutes)

☞ Try not to get caught up in the details of throwing the football. More will come later, as players become developmentally ready.

☞ Go over receiving rules (see page 131).

Goal

Players will get open, receive passes, move downfield, and score.

Description

Repeat game 1.

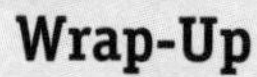

Team Circle (5 minutes)

Key Idea: Responsibility

Gather children into a group. "I want us all to pretend we're eggs. Eggs have shells that can break. What would happen if we bumped into each other as eggs? Right. We would crack and break. Let's move around the field being eggs. Don't bump each other or we'll break!" Continue for about one minute. "We were all careful not to bump each other so that our shells wouldn't break! That was great! You were in charge of, or responsible for, your moving. When we're careful of each other, we're responsible for our space and other players' space. This shows responsibility during practice and games."

Wrap-Up

Make summary comments about practice. Remind players of the next practice day and time.

Practice 3

Warm-Up (10 minutes)

Have the players jog for 3 minutes and then get into a circle. Lead them in five push-ups and jumping jacks.

Fitness Circle (5 minutes)

Key Idea: General fitness

Gather the children into a group. "We all have lungs. Your lungs, like your heart, are in your chest and you can't see them. Unlike your heart, you have two lungs—one on your left side and one on your right side. Your lungs hide right behind your ribs. Where are your ribs? You can feel your ribs on the sides of your chest.

"Your lungs have the job of getting air in and out of your body. Take a deep breath. Look at your chest when you do this. When you breathe in, your lungs fill up with air and your chest lifts up and gets bigger. That is so air can get into your lungs. Now blow the air out. When you do that, your chest gets smaller."

Activity: Deep breathing

"Lie flat on your back. Place your right hand on your abdomen (belly) just below your ribs. Place your left hand on the center of your chest. Take a really deep breath. Breathe in through your nose *and* mouth. When you do this, push your chest outward and upward. Your belly will rise as well. Hold your breath. Let the air out of your lungs by opening your mouth and pulling your abdomen inward. Do this several times. What do you notice?" [Chest gets bigger, I am able to control my breathing, it relaxes me.]

Game 1 (10 minutes)

Goal

Receivers will run routes and get open to receive passes.

Description

Split the players into four teams, two Team As and two Team Bs, on two different parts of the field. Team As begin and remain on offense for the first half of the game; Team Bs are on offense for the second half of the game. The two Team As begin at midfield and move toward opposite goals. On defense, play either zone (one player covers left, one middle,

PURPOSE

To learn a pass pattern

Equipment

- One football for every two players (Nerf ball or youth-size: 10 1/4- to 10 1/2-inch)
- Grass field 30 yards by 60 yards

and one right) or player-to-player (with one player assigned to the quarterback). Receivers are to run however they want in attempting to get open and receive a pass. Rotate offensive players to different positions after each play. The receiver is down where he or she caught the ball (you can opt to allow the receivers to run with the ball and the defenders to touch them with one hand to down them). Award one point for each pass caught.

Coach: How should you hold your hands when catching a ball below the waist?
Players: Put your little fingers together.

Coach: How about above the waist?
Players: Put your thumbs together.

Skill Practice 1 (10 minutes)

1. Introduce, demonstrate, and explain how to *catch the football* (see page 121).
2. Have players practice catching the football in a stationary position.

Description

Pair up players, with each pair having a ball. They play catch, with the throws going to different locations, as called out by you: above the head; below the waist; to the side. (If they aren't able to hit these locations, that's okay; the main point is to practice catching.)

Skill Practice 2 (10 minutes)

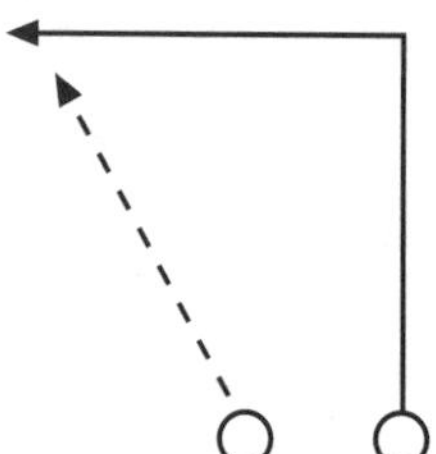

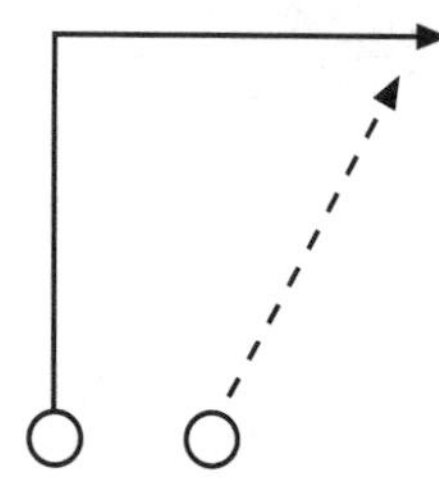

1. Introduce, demonstrate, and explain how to catch the football on the run, using the *square-out pass pattern* (see page 117).
2. Have players practice catching the football using the square-out pass pattern.

Description

Pair up players, with each pair having a ball. The pairs of players then throw each other passes using the square-out pattern.

"Be soft all over."
"Look the ball into your hands."
"Catch the ball with your hands, not with your body."

Practice 3

Game 2 (10 minutes)

Goal

Players will catch the ball while running the square-out pass pattern.

Description

Repeat Game 1, with the receivers running square-outs.

Team Circle (5 minutes)

Key Idea: Responsibility

Gather children into a group. Dump five to six balls out of a mesh ball bag, leaving them where they stop. "Pretend we just finished one activity in practice and we're getting ready to do something else. Everyone walk away from the balls and make a group circle." Pick up the balls, then go to the group. Dump balls out again. "Now come back and you pick up the balls, then go make a circle. Which way makes it faster for me to get to your circle?" Listen to their responses. "What do you think we should do with the balls?" Listen to their responses. Discuss picking up equipment before doing another activity. "We can have more fun and learn more when we work together. That is a shared responsibility between the coach and the players."

Wrap-Up

Make summary comments about practice. Remind players of the next practice day and time.

Variations

Make the games and skill practices easier or harder for the kids by adjusting the difficulty of the passes or the length of the patterns.

☞ Correct hand position and remembering the coach's cues are keys to good pass receiving.

☞ Go over the no-block rule (see page 132).

Practice 4

PURPOSE

To set up the offensive attack

Equipment

- One football for every two players (Nerf ball or youth-size: 10 1/4- to 10 1/2-inch)
- Grass field 30 yards by 60 yards

Warm-Up (10 minutes)

Have the players jog one lap around the field. Lead them in push-ups and jumping jacks. Then pair them up and have them pass to each other.

Fitness Circle (5 minutes)

Key Idea: Cardiorespiratory health and fitness

Equipment: Two cones

Gather the children into a group. "People who play football, run, or swim have hearts and lungs that work really well. That is because our bodies were made to be exercised every day. People who live in some countries have to exercise hard every day just to find or get food. Have you ever heard of people who need to work hard to get food?"

Activity: Running plus breathing and heart rate

"When I tell you to, I want you to run as fast as you can to the cone and back." (The cone is to be placed 50 yards from where you are speaking.) "Do you understand? Ready? Go!" (As the children run, encourage them to run as fast as they can.)

When the children return, tell them, "Think about your heart and lungs. Can you feel your heart pumping faster?" (Some will, some won't.) "Are you breathing faster?" (Some will be able to answer, others will not.) "When your heart beats faster and your lungs breathe deeper and faster, that is a sign that your heart and lungs are getting more exercise. If you do this day after day, your heart and lungs will get stronger."

Game 1 (10 minutes)

Goal

Players will catch passes while running square-outs.

Description

Play games of 3 v 3. On defense, play either zone (one player covers left, one middle, and one right) or player-to-player (with one player assigned to the quarterback). Have receivers run square-outs. The offense starts 30 yards away from the goal and has six passes to at-

Practice 4

tempt to score. Each completion is worth one point; a touchdown is worth six. Switch offense and defense after a touchdown or after six passes, whichever comes first. The offense always begins 30 yards from the goal. The receiver is down where he or she caught the ball (you can opt to allow the receivers to run with the ball and the defenders to touch them with one hand to down them).

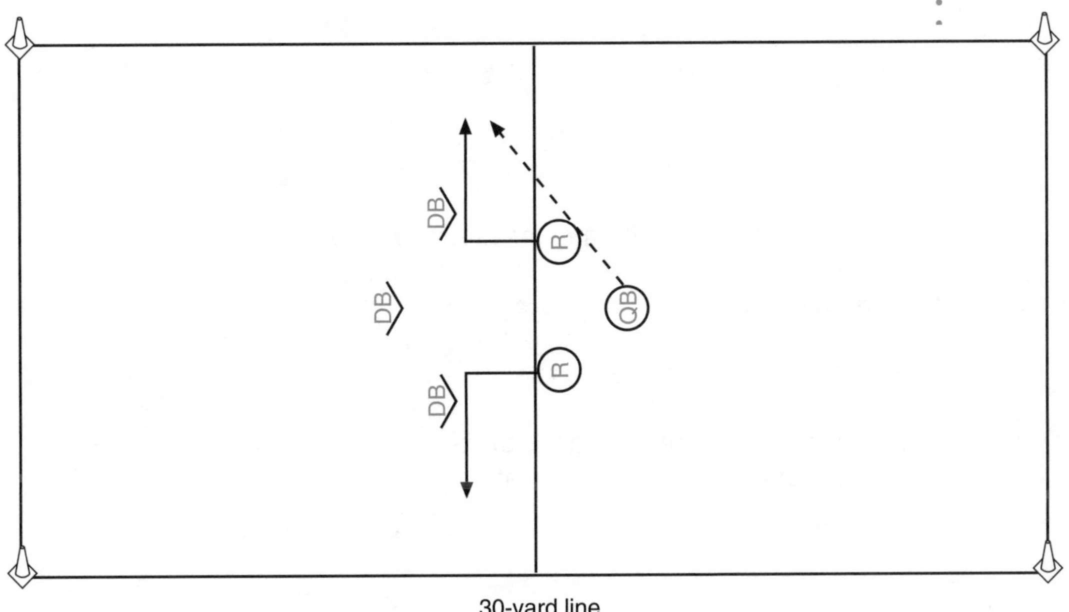

Coach: How should you hold your hands when catching a ball below the waist?
Players: Put your little fingers together.

Coach: How about above the waist?
Players: Put your thumbs together.

Coach: What's another way to get open besides the square-out pattern?
Players: The curl pattern.

Skill Practice 1 (10 minutes)

1. Introduce, demonstrate, and explain how to catch the football on the run, using the *curl pass pattern* (see page 117).
2. Have players practice catching the football using the curl pass pattern.

Description

Divide players into pairs, each pair with one football. One player runs a curl pattern while his or her partner throws a pass. Have receivers run five curls then switch roles so that their partners can run curls.

"Curl back!"
"Proper hand position."
"Tuck the ball away."

Skill Practice 2 (10 minutes)

Review the proper technique for catching the football on the run. Divide players into teams of three—one quarterback and two receivers. Have quarterbacks throw passes to the players running curls and square-outs (you call out the pattern). One receiver per team goes out at a time; on the next pass, the other receiver goes out. After each receiver has gone out three times, rotate positions so that the quarterback becomes a receiver. Check to see if the players are using the correct hand position on each catch.

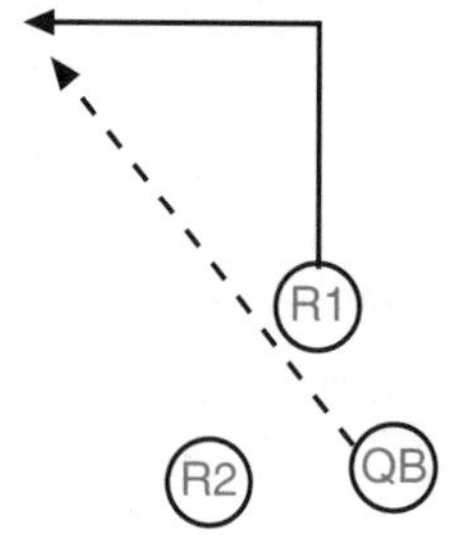

First pass

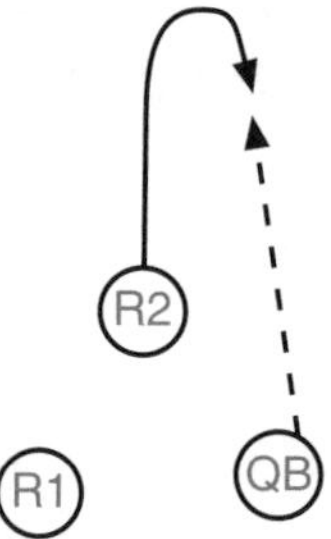

Second pass

"Soft hands!"
"Look the ball into your hands."
"Use your hands to catch, not your body."

Practice 4

Game 2 (10 minutes)

Goal

Players will catch the ball while running the correct pass pattern.

Description

Repeat game 1, with you calling out the pass patterns—square-outs and curls.

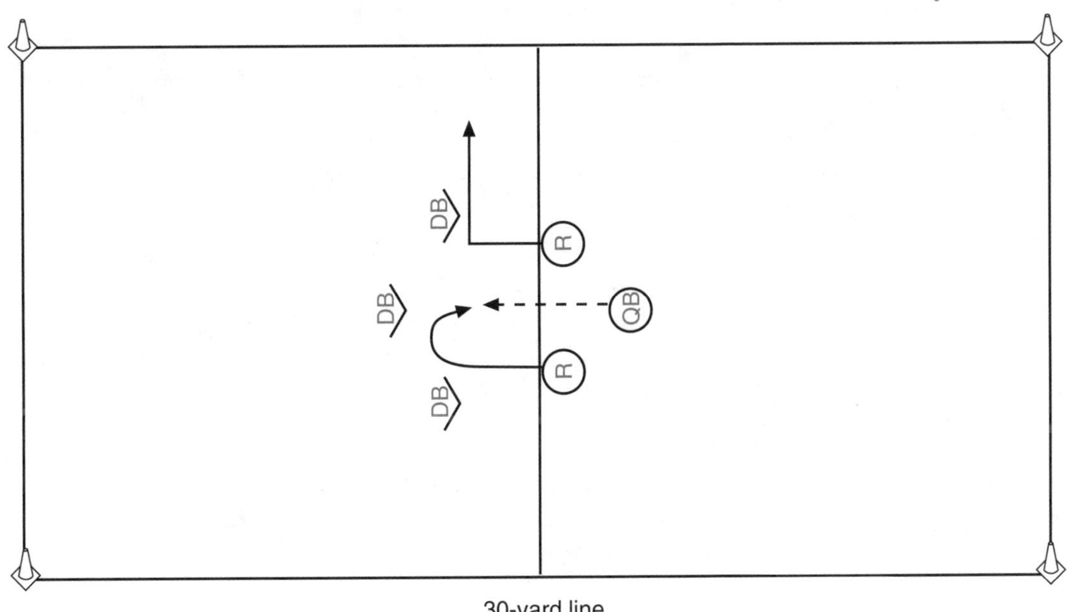

☞ Keeping your eyes on the ball and being soft are keys to good pass receiving.

☞ Go over defensive rules (see page 132).

Team Circle (5 minutes)

Key Idea: Honesty

Gather children into a group. "Can you interfere with pass receivers in flag football? Even if it's an accident? Those of you who think it's okay to commit pass interference, stand to my left. Those who think it's not okay, stand to my right." Wait for children to choose. Then ask them why they chose as they did. "Pass interference, even if it's an accident, is a violation. What should you do if that happens? Those of you who think you should just keep playing, stand to my left; those of you who think you should raise your hand or tell the official, stand to my right." Wait for everyone to finish choosing. "It's important to be honest about committing violations. If you commit pass interference or some other violation, even if nobody sees it, raise your hand or tell the official."

Wrap-Up

Make summary comments about practice. Remind players of the next practice day and time.

Practice 5

Warm-Up (10 minutes)

Have the players run for 2 minutes and then split up into groups of three (quarterback, receiver, defensive back) and play catch, running pass patterns against the defender. Players should rotate so that they play each position.

PURPOSE

To stop offensive progress

Equipment

- One football for every two players (Nerf ball or youth-size: 10 1/4- to 10 1/2-inch)
- Towels or cones to mark zones
- A flag belt (with flags) for each player

Fitness Circle (5 minutes)

Key Idea: Muscle fitness (strength)

Gather the children into a group. "Watch my arm as I make a muscle." (Flex your biceps muscle.) "Now you try it. This is only one of over 600 muscles that you have in your body. These muscles help you walk, play the piano, and do sports. If you didn't have muscles, your bones would fall to the floor. Your muscles get stronger (and sometimes bigger) when you exercise them. Usually bigger muscles mean that you are stronger."

Activity: Push-up

"Here is an exercise that will make your arms stronger. The muscles in your arms need to be developed to play football well. This exercise is called a push-up. Lie on your stomach. Place your hands to the outside of your shoulders with your fingers pointing straight ahead. Push your upper body off the floor, keeping your knees on the floor. You should form a straight line from your head to your knees when you are in this push-up position. Lower your body until your chest almost touches the floor." [Children may try a full push-up (no knee support) if they wish.]

"What muscles does this exercise make stronger?" [The muscles on the backs of the arms.] "Now show me another exercise you know." [Variety demonstrated.]

Game 1 (10 minutes)

Goal

Defenders will pull the offensive player's flag in game situations.

Description

Play two 3 v 3 games simultaneously or one 6 v 6 game. Play either zone or player-to-player (with one player assigned to the quarterback). Call out the routes that receivers should run. Defenders must pull the flag to stop the ball carrier's progress. (If this proves too advanced, use a one-hand tag to down ball carriers.) Start the offense at one goal line and see how far they can advance down the field in six plays. Then switch sides. The new offense begins at a goal line and tries to advance farther down the field than the first offense did.

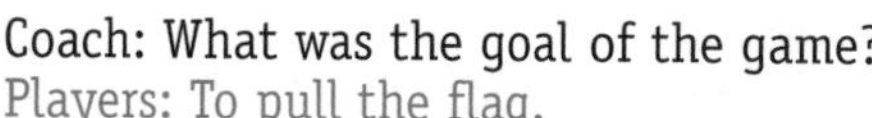

Coach: What was the goal of the game?
Players: To pull the flag.

Coach: What's the best way to pull the flag?
Players: Try to grab it.

Coach: Should you lunge for the runner or let the runner come to you?
Players: Wait for the runner to come to you.

Coach: Should you keep your weight back, on the balls of your feet (indicate what these are), or should you get up on your toes?
Players: Keep your weight on the balls of your feet.

Coach: Good. Let's practice pulling flags.

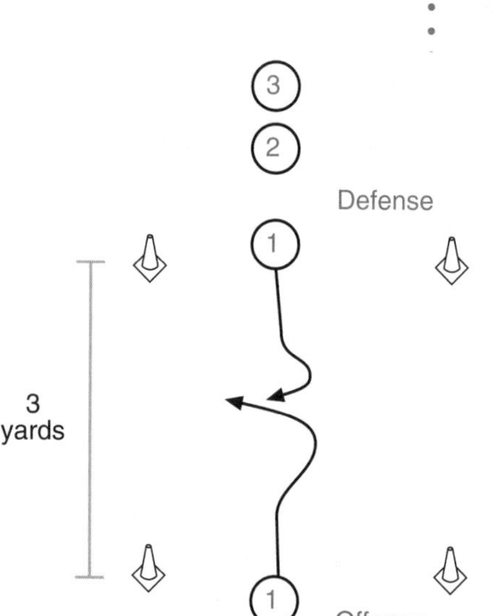

Skill Practice 1 (10 minutes)

1. Introduce, demonstrate, and explain how to *pull the flag* (see page 123).
2. Have players practice pulling flags.

Description

Divide the players into two groups. Within each group, have a line of offensive players and a line of defensive players (three players per line). Mark a zone 3 yards wide by 3 yards long. Have an offensive player run through the zone while a defensive player attempts to pull his or her flag. Those two players then go to the ends of their lines. When each defensive player has had three attempts to pull a flag, switch the offense and defense and continue the skill practice.

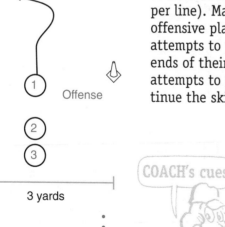

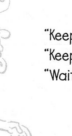

"Keep your feet shoulder-width apart."
"Keep a low center of gravity."
"Wait for the runner to come to you."

Practice 5

Skill Practice 2 (10 minutes)

Repeat skill practice 1, but this time the defensive player begins on his or her back. Toss the ball to the offensive player. With the toss, the defender gets up and attempts to pull the flag off the offensive player before he or she can run through the zone.

Game 2 (10 minutes)

Goal

The offense will make first downs and touchdowns and the defense will stop offensive progress.

Description

Play 6 v 6, with the players putting into play all the skills that they have been taught. Play either zone or player-to-player defense (with one player assigned to the quarterback). Give the offense two points for each first down and six points for each score. The defense must pull the flag to stop the ball carrier. Give the defense two points for each incomplete pass *if it is touched by a defender* and three points for an interception.

☞ Go over the flag-guarding rule (see page 133).

☞ Flag pulling may prove to be too difficult for youngsters this age. If so, revert back to one-hand (or two-hand) touches to down ball carriers.

Team Circle (5 minutes)

Key Idea: Respect

Gather children into a single-file line. "I am going to walk down the line two times. Remember how it feels each time I pass you." Walk down the line and nod to each player. Repeat, but this time tell each player "great game" or "nice play today" and shake his or her hand. "Which time that I passed you made you feel better? Shaking hands and saying 'good game' are important traditions that show we appreciate our opponents' efforts in a game. It shows respect for your opponents." Divide the team in half and have players practice an end-of-game "respect ritual."

Wrap-Up

Remind players of the next practice day and time.

Practice 6

PURPOSE

To learn a new pass pattern

Equipment

- One football for every two players (Nerf ball or youth-size: 10 1/4- to 10 1/2-inch)
- Grass field 30 yards by 60 yards
- A flag belt (with flags) for each player

Warm-Up (10 minutes)

Have the players jog one lap around the field. Choose two quarterbacks to throw to receivers running square-outs and curls. Correct the players when the right pattern is not executed.

Fitness Circle (5 minutes)

Key Idea: Muscle fitness

Gather the children into a group. "Flexibility means how far you can stretch a muscle or how much you can move a joint. What is a joint?" [Where two bones meet.] "If you have good flexibility, there is a better chance you will not hurt your muscles when exercising or doing chores. Good flexibility also helps you do better at sports and playing games. Football players especially need a lot of flexibility to prevent injuries."

Activity: Flexibility

"Today we are going to be rubber-band boys and girls. Reach down your back with one hand and reach up your back with your other hand. Try to touch your fingers. If you can do that, you have flexible arms and shoulders.

"Sit on the floor and put your legs straight in front of you. Bend forward at your waist. How close can you get your face (or forehead) to your knees? If you can almost reach your knees, you have good leg and maybe back flexibility.

"Your muscles must be strong and flexible. That means you can stretch far without hurting yourself. I want to see how flexible you really are. Can you kiss your elbow? Try it." (They will not be able to do so, but they will have fun trying.)

Game 1 (10 minutes)

Goal

Receivers will run routes against defenders and get open to receive passes.

Description

Play 4 v 4; one quarterback and three receivers on offense and four defenders on defense. Rotate teams from offense to defense every three plays. The offense will run "hot" (full speed). The defense will run "cold" (half-speed), playing a zone—two players up front, two playing deep—allowing the offense to catch the ball when patterns are run correctly. The receiver is down where he or she caught the ball (you can opt to allow the receivers to run with the ball and the defenders to either touch them with one hand to down them or practice pulling flags). Receivers should run however they want to in attempting to get open and receive a pass. Count one point for each pass caught.

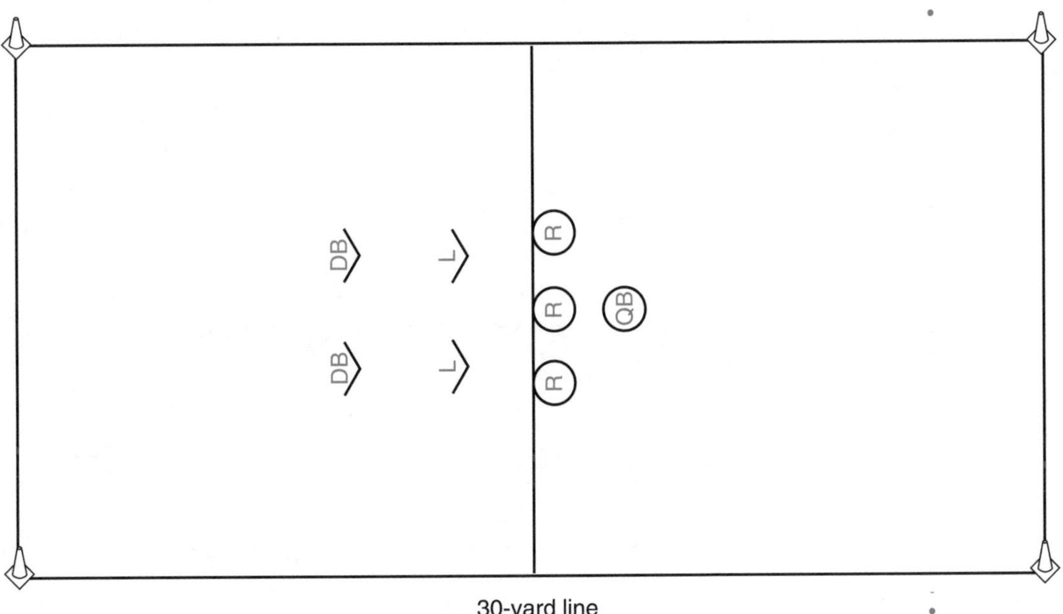

Coach: What was the goal of the game?
Players: To run and get open and catch passes.

Coach: How do you get open?
Players: By running different patterns.

Coach: Let's try a pattern called "the slant."

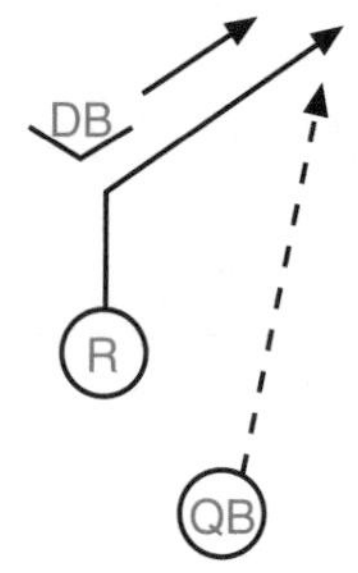

Skill Practice (15 minutes)

1. Introduce, demonstrate, and explain the *slant pattern* (see page 117).
2. Have players practice running the slant pattern.

Description

Split your squad into three-player groups. In each group, there's a quarterback, a receiver, and a defensive back. The receivers run slant patterns and attempt to catch passes. Rotate positions after a receiver has run the route three times.

"Change your speed."
"Change your direction."
"Make good fakes and sharp cuts."

Game 2 (10 minutes)

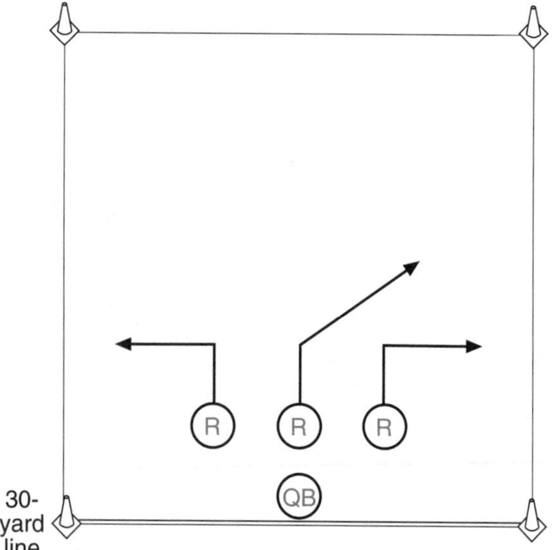

Goal

Players will run pass patterns, move the ball downfield, and score.

Description

Split your squad into three or four teams and place the teams on different quadrants of the field. Each team is on offense; there is no defense. Teams will begin at midfield and work their way downfield by completing passes. Tell wide receivers (the ones on either side of the ball, farthest from the ball) to run square-outs; the others can run either a curl or a slant. The ball is down where caught. Award one point for each completed pass and two points for each touchdown. After each play, rotate players so that someone else plays quarterback.

Practice 6

Team Circle (5 minutes)

Key Idea: Caring

Gather children into a circle. Stand in the middle of the group with a ball. Pass to each child and give them a turn to pass back to you. "I am going to pass the ball. If a pass comes to you, pass the ball back to me." Work around the whole circle. Talk to the children about playing and learning when they come to practice. "Who had a turn to touch the ball?" Wait for their responses. "I made sure everyone had a chance to touch the ball. Raise your hand if it felt good to be able to have a turn. How would you have felt if you did not have a turn?" Listen to their responses. "We need to share the ball and take turns playing different positions so that everyone can learn and play. Sharing and taking turns shows you care."

Wrap-Up

Make summary comments about practice. Remind players of the next practice day and time.

Variation

To make the games harder, play defense against the offense in game 2.

☞ Being able to get open is a key to good pass receiving.

☞ Go over running rules (see page 131).

Practice 7

PURPOSE

To run effective pass patterns and get open

Equipment

- One football for every two players (Nerf ball or youth-size: 10 1/4- to 10 1/2-inch)
- Grass field 30 yards by 60 yards
- A flag belt (with flags) for each player

Warm-Up (10 minutes)

Have the players run for 2 minutes. Have the kids throw passes to each other, taking turns being quarterbacks and receivers.

Fitness Circle (5 minutes)

Key Idea: Training and conditioning

Gather the children into a group. "What do people like football players, runners, and gymnasts do before they play their sports or run races?" [They stretch, warm up, do these kinds of exercises . . . .] "Getting ready to exercise is sometimes called warming up. Warming up helps prevent injuries, gets athletes thinking about their sports, and helps get their hearts and lungs ready for exercise. What exercises do football players do before playing?" [Stretching, running, catching punts, kicking balls, throwing and catching balls, practicing blocking.]

Activity: Warm-up exercises

"Here are some getting-ready exercises for flag football" (see pages 140-141).

Game 1 (20 minutes)

Goal

Players will run routes that will get them open.

Description

Play two simultaneous 3 v 3 games. Have receivers run various routes against defenders with you telling the offense (so the defense doesn't hear) the routes. On defense, play either zone (one player covers left, one middle, and one right) or player-to-player. Have the offense remain on offense for 5 minutes, then switch offense and defense. Give two points when the intended receiver runs his or her route correctly, and add a point if the receiver makes the catch. The receiver is down where he or she caught the ball (you can opt to allow the receivers to run with the ball and the defenders to either touch them with one hand to down them or to practice pulling flags).

Practice 7

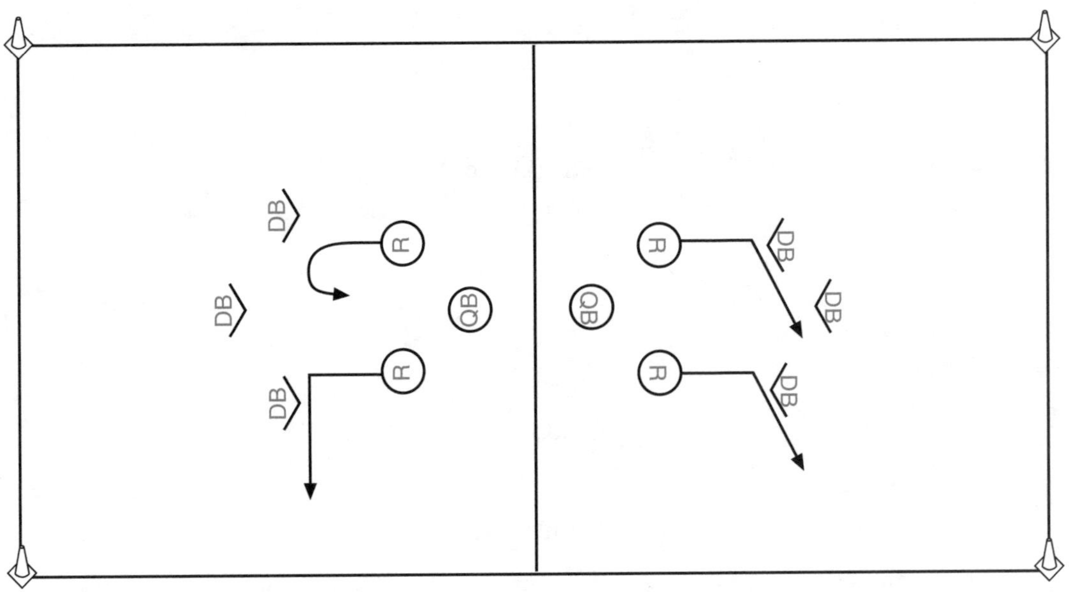

Coach: What was the goal of the game?
Players: To get open to catch a pass.

Coach: How can you get open to catch a pass?
Players: By running specific patterns.

Skill Practice (10 minutes)

Split your squad into three-player groups. In each group, there's a quarterback, a receiver, and a defensive back. The same receiver runs each of three routes—the curl, the square-out, and the slant—and attempts to catch passes. Rotate positions after a receiver has run all three routes.

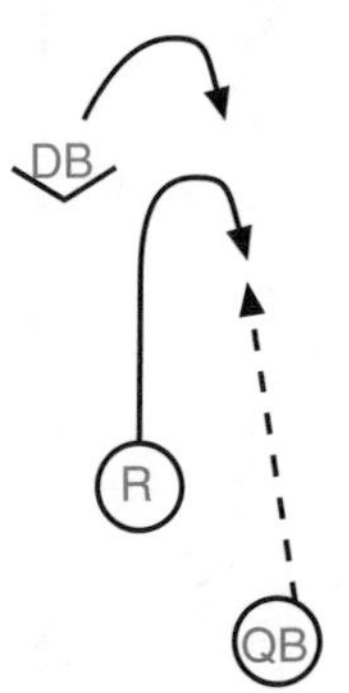

Play 1

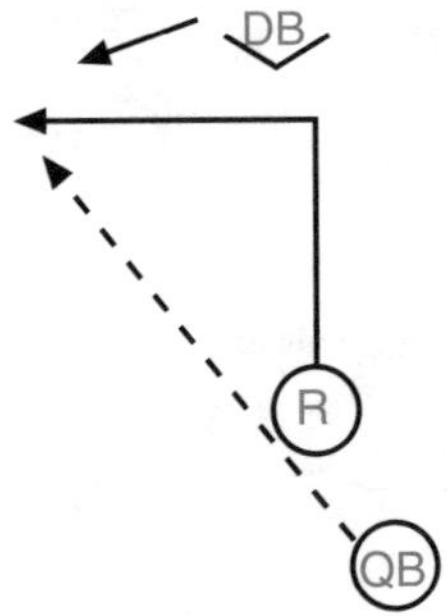

Play 2

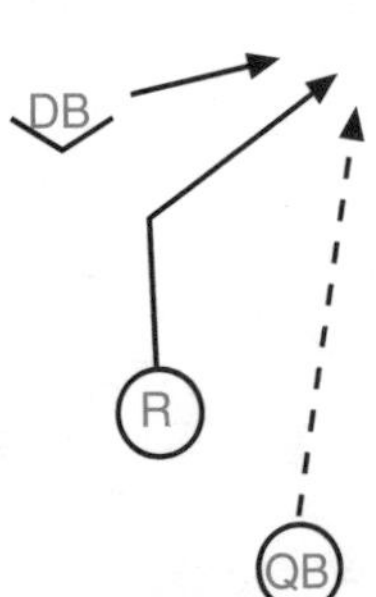

Play 3

"Run an exact pattern!"
"Change your speed and direction."

Game 2 (15 minutes)

Goal

Receivers will run correct routes and make catches.

Description

Divide the players into three teams of four and have the quarterbacks throw to the receivers with no defense. Place the teams in different quadrants of the field, all starting at midfield (two teams will be going the same direction down the field). Have the two outside receivers run square-outs and the inside receiver run a curl. Award a point to each receiver who runs the correct pattern and a point for each catch made.

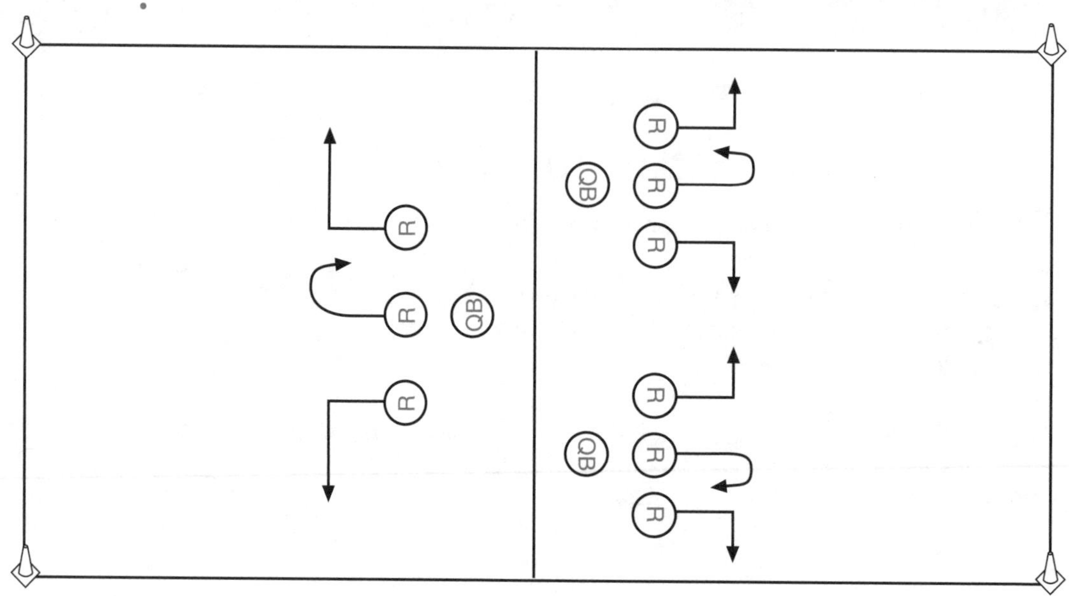

Practice 7

Team Circle (5 minutes)

Key Idea: Caring

Gather the children into a group. "Let's pretend we're playing a flag football game. Watch what I do with the ball." Tell a child in the group that you're passing to him. Make a bad pass. "That pass wasn't very good, was it? What would you say to me so that I don't feel bad about the pass?" As children respond, have each player who makes a supportive comment stand beside you. If players make comments that aren't supportive, encourage them to change their words to become more supportive; after they have changed the words, they join their teammates beside you. "It's very important to support your teammates, especially when they make mistakes. Saying something that makes someone feel good shows you care."

Wrap-Up

Make summary comments about practice. Remind players of the next practice day and time.

COACH's points

☞ Playing smart is a large part of being a good pass receiver.

☞ Go over the offsides rule (see page 132).

Practice 8

PURPOSE

To learn a new pass pattern

Equipment

- One football for every two players (Nerf ball or youth-size: 10 1/4- to 10 1/2-inch)
- Grass field 30 yards by 60 yards
- A flag belt (with flags) for each player

Warm-Up (10 minutes)

Have the players jog one lap around the field and then come back and run the pass patterns they have learned. Correct the players when their hand positions or routes are not done correctly. Lead them in stretches for their legs and arms.

Fitness Circle (5 minutes)

Key Idea: Safety

Gather the children into a group. "A room has four walls, a floor, and a ceiling. Between the walls, ceiling, and floor is called 'space.' You have space, too. It is called personal space. If we all started playing football or doing exercises right now, some of us might bump into each other and get hurt. If you spread out, each of you would have enough personal space, or space you have to share with everyone else."

Activity: Finding your personal space

"Now let's see what personal space is. Put your arms out to your sides as far as possible. Now stretch them upward, backward, and in front of you as far as possible. That is your personal space. That is because you can swing your arms without hitting anyone.

"Now let's walk around the field without bumping into anyone. Let's run without running into anyone. Now swing your arms without running into anyone. You have learned what personal space is. When I say, 'Watch your personal space,' that means don't run into anyone."

Practice 8

Game 1 (15 minutes)

Goal

Players will run good pass routes.

Description

Play two 3 v 3 games. Have receivers run various routes against defenders with you telling the offense (so that the defense doesn't hear) the routes. On defense, play either zone (one player covers left, one middle, and one right) or player-to-player. Have the offense remain on offense for five plays, then switch offense and defense. Continue to rotate in this fashion. Give two points per catch—if the route was run correctly. The receiver is down where he or she caught the ball (you can opt to allow the receivers to run with the ball and the defenders to either touch them with one hand to down them or practice pulling flags).

Coach: What was the goal of the game?
Players: To run correct pass routes.

Coach: Why is it important to run the correct route?
Players: So the quarterback knows where to look for receivers.

Coach: We've learned curls, square-outs, and slants. What's another way you can get open?
Players: The streak pattern.

Skill Practice (15 minutes)

1. Introduce, demonstrate, and explain the *streak pattern* (see page 117).
2. Have players practice running the streak pattern.

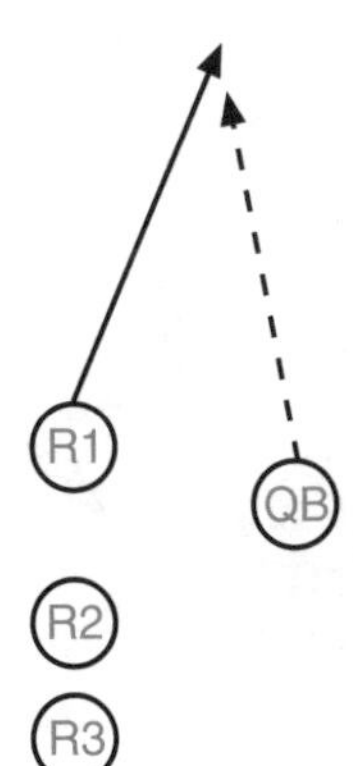

Description

Split your squad into four-player groups. In each group, there's a quarterback and three receivers, lined up so that one receiver at a time will go out. Have two footballs available for each quarterback. The receivers run streak patterns and attempt to catch passes. After the three receivers have gone out for a pass, one of them becomes the quarterback, and the quarterback becomes a receiver as the skill practice continues.

Game 2 (15 minutes)

Goal

Players will run various patterns and get open to catch passes.

Description

Play two simultaneous 3 v 3 games. Call the pattern before each play (streak, slant, square-out, or curl). The defense should play a "cold" defense, playing either zone (one player covers left, one middle, and one right) or player-to-player. The receiver is down where he or she caught the ball (you can opt to allow the receivers to run with the ball and the defenders to either touch them with one hand to down them or practice pulling flags). The offense will receive a point when the receiver who is passed to runs the right route and another point if that receiver makes a catch.

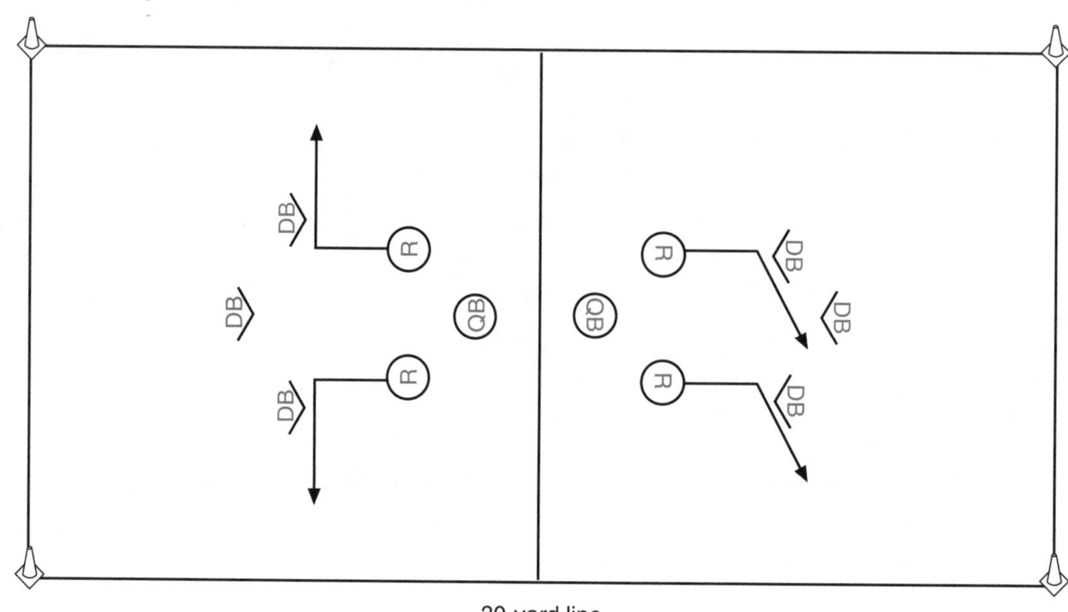

☞ Everyone must know the patterns and run routes precisely so that the quarterback can find and throw to an open receiver.

☞ Go over the pass interference rule (see page 132).

"Make cuts believable."

"Run your route!"

Practice 8

Team Circle (5 minutes)

Key Idea: Responsibility

Gather the children. Have all the balls nearby. Privately tell two children that you are going to ask them to help pick up the balls and you want them to ignore your request. Then ask two other children to begin picking up balls and putting them in the ball bag or bringing them over to you. Then ask the two children that you've alerted to ignore you to help pick up. Then ask the group which kids were being responsible, the first pair or the second pair. Let the kids know you instructed the second pair not to help out. "When you listen to me and help out, you're being responsible to me and to your teammates. A big part of being on a team is being responsible by listening and pitching in."

Wrap-Up

Make summary comments about practice. Remind players of the next practice day and time.

Practice 9

☞ PURPOSE

To run effective pass patterns and get open

Equipment

- One football for every two players (Nerf ball or youth-size: 10 1/4- to 10 1/2-inch)
- Grass field 30 yards by 60 yards
- A flag belt (with flags) for each player

Warm-Up (10 minutes)

Have the player jog for two minutes. Then have them pair up and play catch, running the pass patterns they learned in previous practices.

Fitness Circle (5 minutes)

Key Idea: Healthy habits

Equipment: Footballs (one for every four children), two different-colored hoops for each team of four. (If possible, each child would have a football and two colored hoops.)

Gather the children into a group. "When you exercise and it is hot, you may sweat too much. When that happens, you lose a lot of water. That means you have to put water or liquid back inside of you. What do you usually drink when you are thirsty?" [Soda pop, water, milk, juice, fruit drinks.] "It is best when you have sweat a lot to drink water. That is the easiest and least expensive thing to drink. When you need something that gives you vitamins and minerals and powers you up, drink milk and fruit juices and not soda pop. Soda pop has lots of sugar and no vitamins or minerals."

Activity: Football beverage toss

Divide the children into teams of four. In front of each team, place a yellow hoop (representing water) and a red hoop (representing soda pop); other colors will do. Tell the children their job when they step to the front of the line is to toss the football into the yellow hoop (or water)—the preferred drink. If all four children do this, their team wins—all teams can be winners. If the ball lands in a red hoop or doesn't get into the yellow hoop, the child gets to toss the ball again.

Game 1 (10 minutes)

Goal

Players will get open using various pass routes.

Description

Play two 3 v 3 games. Have receivers run various routes against defenders with you telling the offense (so that the defense doesn't hear) the routes. On defense, play either zone (one player covers left, one middle, and one right) or player-to-player. Have the offense remain on offense for five plays, then switch offense and defense. Continue to rotate in this fashion. Give two points per catch—if the route was run correctly. The receiver is down where he or she caught the ball (you can opt to allow the receivers to run with the ball and the defenders to either touch them with one hand to down them or practice pulling flags).

Coach: What was the goal of the game?
Players: To run correct pass routes.

Coach: Why is it important to run the correct route?
Players: Because the quarterback must know where everyone is on the field to be able to complete the pass.

Skill Practice (15 minutes)

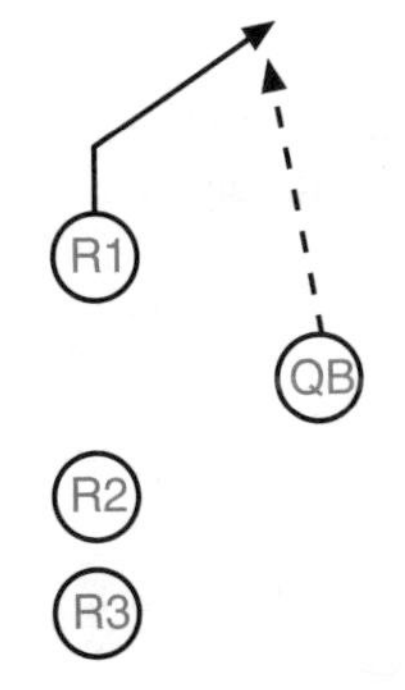

Split your squad into four-player groups. In each group, there's a quarterback and three receivers, lined up so that one receiver at a time will go out. Have two footballs available for each quarterback. You call the pass pattern for each receiver. After the three receivers have gone out for a pass, one of them becomes the quarterback, and the quarterback becomes a receiver as the skill practice continues.

"Run your route."
"Good fakes and sharp cuts!"

Game 2 (15 minutes)

Goal

Players will correctly run routes with pressure on the quarterback.

Description

Divide the team into three groups, each with a quarterback, two receivers, and a rusher. All three groups run the play at the same time. You call out the routes for the receivers and the quarterbacks throw to one of the receivers. The rushers put pressure on the quarterbacks after a 5-second count (given by you or your assistant). Rotate players—the receiver who was thrown the pass becomes the rusher; the rusher becomes the quarterback; the other receiver remains a receiver until he or she is thrown a pass.

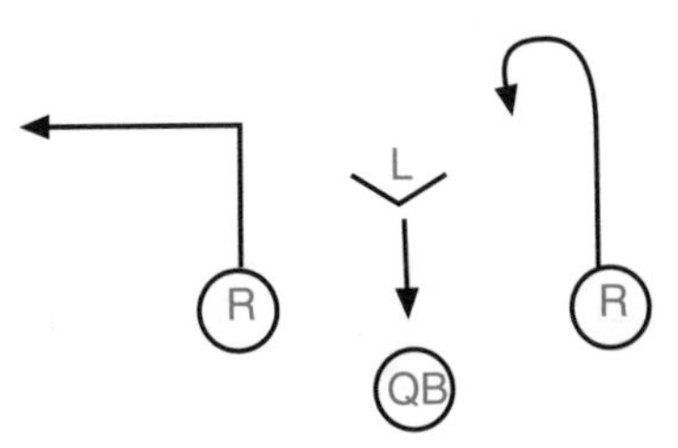

Variation

To make game 2 harder, cut out one receiver and add a defensive back (so that you have a quarterback and receiver against a rusher and a defensive back). But use caution in making the game too competitive too early, because the players may forget about learning the skill and just worry about scoring.

☞ Running correct routes will spread the field and make it easy for the quarterback to find the open receiver. Receivers need to run their routes quickly so that the quarterback can get rid of the ball before being tagged by the defense.

☞ Go over the illegal rushing rule (see page 132).

Team Circle (5 minutes)

Key Idea: Responsibility

Gather children into a circle. Stand in the center of the circle with a ball. Ask children to call to you and raise their hand if they are in a good position for a pass. Run with the ball inside the circle, but do not pass to anyone. Continue for about 1 minute. "Did I share the ball with anyone?" Wait for their responses. "Do you think that is good teamwork? What *is* good teamwork?" Listen to their responses. Repeat the activity, but this time pass to players who call and raise their hand. "Teamwork is when all players are working together, not just keeping the ball to themselves. Responsible team members get in position to receive a good pass. They don't always pass to the same person. And they always work hard."

Wrap-Up

Make summary comments about practice. Remind players of the next practice day and time.

Practice 10

Warm-Up (10 minutes)

Have the players jog one lap around the field and then come back and run pass patterns. Lead them in jumping jacks and stretches for their legs and arms.

Fitness Circle (5 minutes)

Key Idea: Healthy habits (snacks)

Gather the children into a group. "A snack is any food you eat between meals. Snacks include such things as an apple, a cookie, or chips. Any food (a bowl of cereal or a sandwich) eaten between meals is a snack. There are good and bad snacks. 'Good' snacks are nutritious and make you healthy and strong. Any food can be bad if you eat it too close to meal time and then you don't eat much for dinner. To snack right, do the following:

- Snack two hours or more before a meal.
- Eat small snacks and make sure you have room for dinner.
- Snack only when hungry.
- Choose snacks that are good for you."

Activity: Favorite foods

"When I say a food, tell me if you like it by jumping up and down. If you don't like the food, make a frown. If you think the food is good for you, run in place."

Donuts	Chocolate cake
Peanuts	Milk
Peaches	Apple juice
String beans	Fish
French fries	Chicken

PURPOSE

To cover pass receivers

Equipment

- One football for every two players (Nerf ball or youth-size: 10 1/4- to 10 1/2-inch)
- Grass field 30 yards by 60 yards
- A flag belt (with flags) for each player

Practice 10 (cont'd)

Game 1 (10 minutes)

Goal

Players will cover pass receivers and prevent them from catching passes.

Description

Play 2 v 2 games on different quadrants of the field—a quarterback and a receiver against two defensive backs. The defense can put double coverage on the receiver or choose to rush a player. Each offense starts at midfield and works its way toward the goal line (two going one way, the other two going the other direction).

The offense gets six pass plays, then the teams rotate from offense to defense and vice versa. Call out pass routes for the offenses to run (call them out so that all four offenses can hear the play). The receiver is down where he or she caught the ball (you can opt to allow the receivers to run with the ball and the defenders to either touch them with one hand to down them or practice pulling flags). For each incomplete pass that falls to the ground untouched by the defense, give the defense one point.

For each incomplete pass that *is* touched by the defense, give two points. Give three points for an interception. Take away a point from the defense if a pass is caught.

Once the offense has had six plays, teams switch sides, and the new offenses begin at midfield.

Coach: What was the goal of the game?
Players: To cover the receivers.

Coach: How do you do that?
Players: By using good positioning and staying with the receiver.

Skill Practice 1 (10 minutes)

1. Introduce, demonstrate, and explain how to *cover receivers* (see pages 124-125).
2. Have your players practice the proper footwork needed for covering receivers.

Description

Line players up and stand in front of them holding the football. Point to different directions on the field (back, forward, right, and left) and have the kids run with the proper footwork as they change direction.

Practice 10

Skill Practice 2 (10 minutes)

Divide the players into two groups, each with one quarterback and two single-file lines: one of receivers, the other of defenders. Call out routes for pass receivers. Help defenders line up at the proper distance. They should use good footwork and cut to the ball at the right time.

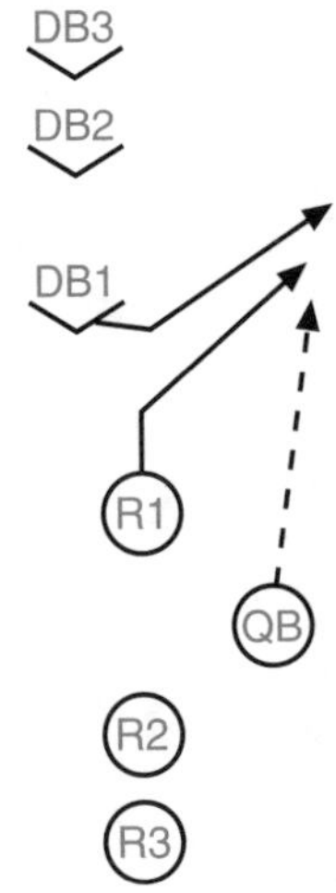

"Stick with the receiver!"
"Look for the ball when the receiver looks for the ball."

Game 2 (10 minutes)

Goal

Defenders will not allow passes to be completed.

Description

Play 6 v 6, playing either a zone or player-to-player defense. If you play a zone, instruct the defense to have two players on the line and four players playing in a line straight across in the defensive backfield, each covering the area in front and behind them. The offense uses the pass routes that they have learned. Play a regulation game, with Team A beginning on offense at the 20-yard line and continuing on as long as they make first downs. Give one point for each first down and six points for a touchdown for the offense. For the defense, award one point for each incomplete pass that falls to the ground untouched by the defense; two points for each incomplete pass that *is* touched by the defense; and three points for each interception.

☞ Defenders should keep receivers in front of them and never turn their backs on them.

☞ Go over the defensive holding rule (see page 132).

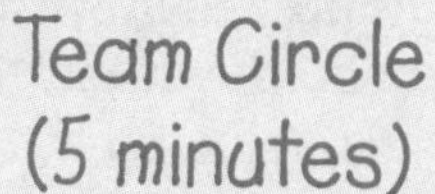

Team Circle (5 minutes)

Key Idea: Keeping perspective

Gather the children into a group. "What did you most enjoy learning about in flag football this season?" Listen to their responses. "Players who thought they tried their best to learn, stand to my left. Players who think they had fun this season, stand to my right. Both of those are important. You should try your best and have fun no matter what happens during the season. The most important thing in flag football is to have fun playing with friends and to learn new skills. I think you all did that! Next year is another chance to have fun, learn new skills, and make new friends!"

Wrap-Up

Make summary comments about what everyone learned over the season. Encourage players to come back next year!

chapter 7

Practice Plans for 6- to 7-Year-Olds

This chapter contains 10 practice plans to use with your 6- and 7-year-old YMCA Rookies flag football players. Before we get to those plans, though, we'll explain the modifications to the game that are used in YMCA Rookies play and give you a quick overview of what's in the practice plans and how they are to be used.

Game Modifications

YMCA Rookies play 6 v 6 games. This speeds up the game and gives kids more opportunities to be involved in the play. Have no more than 12 players on a team.

The field is also smaller than regulation; we recommend a 30-yard by 60-yard field. Again, to keep kids active and to give them more touches of the ball and opportunities to learn, you will see that we quite often recommend having two 3 v 3 games going at once, on separate halves of the field, or having three-player teams performing games and skill practices in separate quadrants of the field. We highly recommend you have at least one assistant coach to help you watch and instruct the players. Encourage parents to help you; the more assistants you have, the more attention each child can get.

Another modification is in the ball itself: we recommend using either a Nerf ball or a youth-size ball (10 1/4 to 10 1/2 inches). If you do try the youth-size ball and find that your players are having trouble gripping or throwing it, be ready to switch to the Nerf ball.

Many of the rules for flag football have been adapted to make them more appropriate for the age and skill level of 6- and 7-year-olds. For example, at this level blocking is not allowed; kickoffs and punting do not take place; there are no running plays; and all offensive players are eligible to receive forward passes. See chapter 9 for more on flag football rules.

Practice Plan Organization

Each plan contains the following sections:

- Purpose
- Equipment
- Warm-Up
- Fitness Circle
- Game 1
- Skill Practice(s)
- Game 2
- Team Circle

Purpose focuses on what you want to teach your players during that practice; it is your main theme for that day. *Equipment* notes what you'll need on hand for that practice (and the size of the field). The *Warm-Up* section gives you 5 to 10 minutes of warm-up activities. This segment will be followed by 5 minutes of the *Fitness Circle*, during which you briefly talk with players about an idea that relates to health or fitness. Then, in *Game 1*, you'll play a game that puts your players in a game-like situation and introduces them to the main tactic or skill that you want them to learn that day.

Then, using the games approach as described in chapter 4, you'll guide your players through a short question-and-answer session that leads to the *Skill Practice.* Here you will have one or two skill practices in which you will teach players the tactic or skill and then conduct a fun drill for them to practice that skill. Remember to use the IDEA approach to teaching skills, as described in chapter 4. (Note that in some games we say play a "hot" defense or a "cold" defense. A "hot" defense is one that is going all-out, trying its hardest to stop the offense. A "cold" defense is one that is playing at about half speed, in more of a "contain" situation—perhaps putting light pressure on the quarterback, but not trying to down him or her, or playing a bit off the receivers, allowing them to make catches and then closing in on them.)

Chapter 8 contains descriptions of all the tactics and skills, so a page reference will be given to guide you to the appropriate description there. The introduction, demonstration, and explanation should be very brief to fit young children's short attention spans. As the players practice, you attend to individual children, guiding them with *Coach's Cues* (which are provided through the practice plans) or further demonstration.

After the skill practices, you will go on to *Game 2* and have the kids play another game to let them use the skills they just learned and to see how those skills fit into the context of a game. We provide *Coach's Points* for you to help your players focus on the most important points. And for many practices we provide *Variations* to give you ideas on how to modify the games to make them easier or more challenging, based on your observations of your players' skill levels.

The practice concludes with a *Team Circle*, which focuses on character development. You take about 5 minutes to talk *with* your players about some aspect of the game that relates to one of the four core values—caring, honesty, respect, and responsibility. Following this, you wrap up the practice with a reminder of the next practice day and time and a preview of what will be taught in that next practice.

A note about Fitness and Team Circles—these times are meant to be true discussions, not lectures where you do all the talking and the kids do all the listening. Ask the questions provided and wait for your players to respond. Don't feed them the answers that we provide; these answers are only meant to help you guide the discussion. The kids' wording of answers doesn't have to match what we give here; that wording is presented for your benefit, so you know where to guide them. Your role in team circles is as much to ask questions and get players to respond as it is to dole out information.

The plans in this chapter, combined with the information in the rest of this book, should give you everything you need to lead practices. Just remember to be patient and caring as you work on skills. Kids will progress at different rates, and it's more important that they learn the sport in a positive way than it is that they learn quickly.

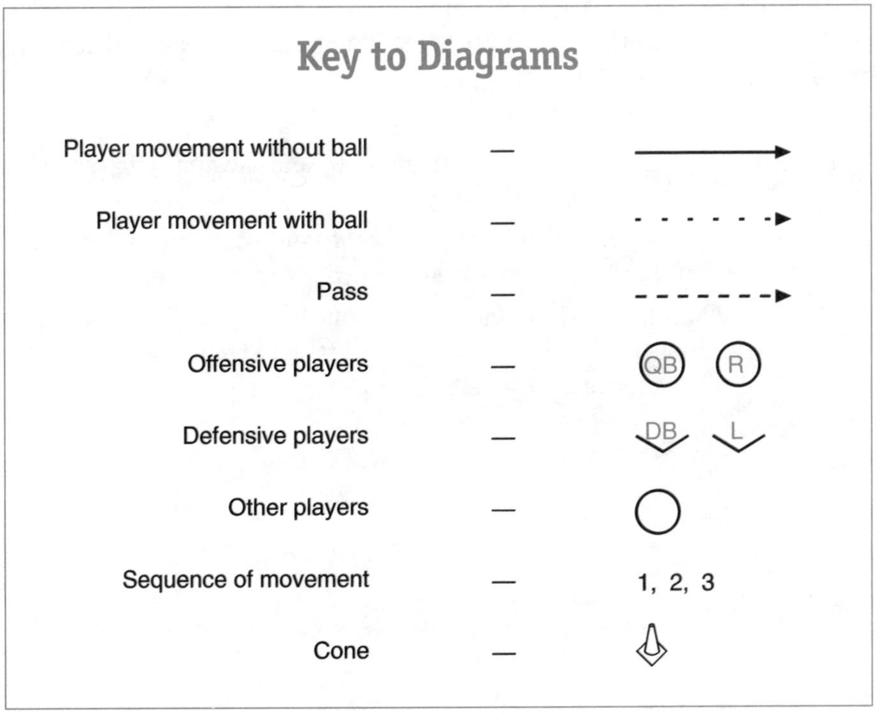

Key to Diagrams

Player movement without ball	—	——————►
Player movement with ball	—	· · · · · · ·►
Pass	—	- - - - - - - -►
Offensive players	—	(QB) (R)
Defensive players	—	DB L
Other players	—	○
Sequence of movement	—	1, 2, 3
Cone	—	

Practice 1

☞ PURPOSE

To learn basic offensive skills

Equipment

- One football for every two players (Nerf ball or youth-size: 10 1/4-to 10 1/2-inch)
- Grass field 30 yards by 60 yards

Warm-Up (5 minutes)

Begin each practice with 5 to 10 minutes of warm-up activities to get players loosened up and ready to go. Have the kids jog one lap around the field and get into a circle. Lead them in jumping jacks and stretches for their legs and arms.

Fitness Circle (5 minutes)

Following the warm-up, gather the players and briefly discuss the fitness concept for that practice.

Key Idea: General fitness

Gather the children together. "Your heart (which is as big as your fist and is located in the center of your chest) pushes blood throughout your body through blood vessels (arteries and veins). Your heart must pump more than 100,000 times a day! That means your heart works without any rest (except between beats)."

Activity: Open-close fist

"Let's see how amazing our hearts are. Place your fist near your chest and open and close your fist as I am doing." (Open and close your fist about 90 times a minute. After a minute or less, the children's hands will start to get tired.) "Is your hand getting tired like mine is?" [A lot of comments and groans.] "As you open and close your fist, think about your heart. Your heart is special. Take care of it with lots of exercise, healthy eating, and plenty of rest."

Ask the children these questions:

- "How did your hand/fist feel after opening and closing your fist 50 to 90 times?" [Tired, hard, achy.]
- "After thinking about your fist and what you just tried to do with it, tell me what you think of your heart now." [Amazing, cool, tough.]
- "What do you think happens to your heart when you play football?" [Heart goes faster, heart gets tired, heart helps you play well.]

Practice 1

Game 1 (10 minutes)

Following the Fitness Circle, get the kids playing a game. Then interrupt each game with a time of questions and answers, with you asking the questions and your players providing the answers (about what the goal of the game was and what skills and tactics they needed to perform to succeed in the game). For many games, we provide diagrams or figures showing how the game is played. We also often provide coaching points for you to pass along to your players during the games.

Goal

Players will move downfield and score.

Description

Play two simultaneous 3 v 3 games. On defense, play player-to-player. The offense starts at midfield and moves downfield in a nonstop passing game—no huddles, no plays, just receivers moving downfield and catching the ball. They are down where they catch it, and the receiver who caught the ball becomes the quarterback, as his or her two teammates immediately go out for passes farther down the field. The defense becomes the offense on an interception or incomplete pass—otherwise the offense keeps moving down the field until they score, so long as they keep completing passes. (You may want to allow the offense to have three incomplete passes before the ball changes hands; keep the game moving, but don't make it too confusing for the players.) Give one point for each completed pass and six points for each touchdown.

Coach: What's the goal of this game?
Players: To move down the field and score.

Coach: How do you do that?
Players: By throwing the ball so the receivers can catch it.

Coach: And how do you do that?
Players: By using the right grip and arm motion.

You'll follow game 1 with one or more skill practices, during which you'll introduce, demonstrate, and explain a skill or tactic, and then attend to your players as they practice it. The question-and-answer session, in which your players tell you what skills and tactics they need to be successful in the game, leads directly to the skill practice. We often provide coaching points with the skill practices; pass these points along to your players. We also give you cues—phrases you can use to help your players focus on the task at hand—in many skill practices and games.

Skill Practice 1 (10 minutes)

1. Introduce, demonstrate, and explain how to *throw the football* (see page 120).
2. Have players practice throwing.

Description

Players in pairs play catch, standing about 3 yards apart. Have them hold the ball high for good rotation and release.

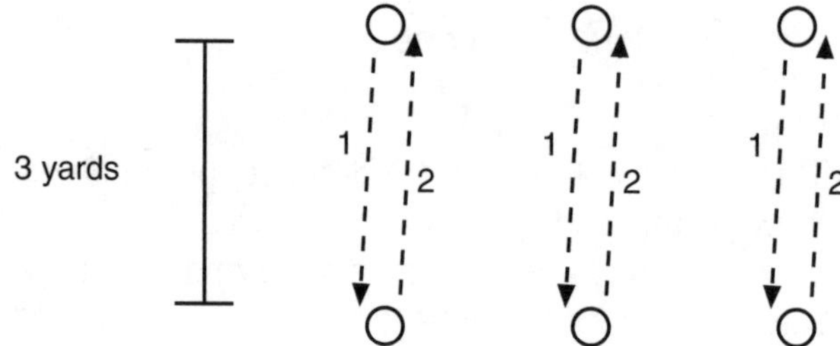

"Spread your fingers on the ball."
"Hold the ball behind your ear."
"Snap your wrist!"

Skill Practice 2 (10 minutes)

Pair up players and have them kneel facing each other about 3 yards apart. They throw 10 balls while on the right knee then switch and throw 10 balls while on the left knee. This will develop arm strength and wrist snap.

"Keep the ball high."
"Throw accurately and hard."

Game 2 (15 minutes)

Goal

Players will pass downfield and score.

Description

Repeat game 1.

☞ Make sure the kids are relaxed and are having fun throwing the football.

☞ Go over passing rules (see page 131).

Team Circle (5 minutes)

Conclude practice by gathering your players and discussing a character development concept. These aren't lectures; you want your players' active participation in these discussions. Following the discussions, wrap up the practice with a few comments.

Key Idea: Four core values

Gather the children into a circle with one ball. "Everyone hand the ball to the person next to you until it makes it around the whole circle." After the ball has gone around the circle one time, have it passed to you. "We play flag football to be more healthy and fit, but it also teaches us to become good teammates and good people. This season we will talk about four qualities of a good person and teammate: caring, honesty, respect, and responsibility. Our team needs to have all of these qualities in our practices and games. Remember that we can't be a team without each of you doing your part. Let's pass the ball to each other and say one of the core values before you pass. This will help you remember to use all four of the qualities so that we can work together."

Wrap-Up

Make summary comments about practice. Remind players of the next practice day and time.

Practice 2

PURPOSE

To learn basic offensive skills

Equipment

- One football for every two players (Nerf ball or youth-size: 10 1/4- to 10 1/2-inch)
- Grass field 30 yards by 60 yards
- Six hula hoops

Warm-Up (5 minutes)

Have the kids jog for 2 minutes and then lead them in stretches for their arms and legs.

Fitness Circle (5 minutes)

Key Idea: General fitness

Gather the children together. "You have a left lung and a right lung in your chest. Each lung is are about the length of a small banana and about the size of two small bananas together. Your lungs have the job of getting air in and out of your body. When you breathe air into your lungs, your lungs get bigger because they are holding air. When you blow the air out of your lungs, your chest gets smaller. You breathe in and out about 12 to 20 times in a minute. The number of times you breathe is called your breathing rate."

Activity: Breathing—nose and mouth

"It is possible to breathe through either just your nose or just your mouth. Try it. Hold you nose shut and open your mouth. Breathe. Now close your mouth and breathe through your nose. Breathe. Do you notice anything different?" (Usually the mouth is easier to breathe through than the nose, although through the nose is preferred.)

Game 1 (10 minutes)

Goal

Players will move downfield and score by throwing accurate passes to teammates.

Description

Play two simultaneous 3 v 3 games. On defense, play player-to-player. The offense starts at midfield and moves downfield in a nonstop passing game—no huddles, no plays, just receivers moving downfield and catching the ball. They are down where they catch it, and the receiver who caught the ball becomes the quarterback, as his or her two teammates immediately go out for passes farther down the field. The defense becomes the offense on an interception or incomplete pass—otherwise

Practice 2

the offense keeps moving down the field until they score, so long as they keep completing passes. (You may want to allow the offense to have three incomplete passes before the ball changes hands; keep the game moving, but don't make it too confusing for the players.) Give one point for each completed pass and six points for each touchdown.

Coach: What was the goal of the game?
Players: To throw accurate passes and score.

Coach: How do you throw accurate passes?
Players: Throw smooth and easy; the ball rolls off your fingers.

Coach: Why did some teams have trouble scoring?
Players: The receivers ran too far away from the quarterback.

Coach: Is it better to use short passes or long passes?
Players: Short passes so the quarterback can get the ball to the receiver.

Skill Practice 1 (10 minutes)

Put players into pairs, with players in each pair standing 5 yards apart. One player holds a hula hoop to the side, as a target for his or her partner to throw through. The player holding the hoop tosses the ball back and continues to hold the hoop until his or her partner has had five throws. Then they switch positions and the second player throws through the hoop. Players score a point for each ball that they throw in the air through the appropriate hula hoop.

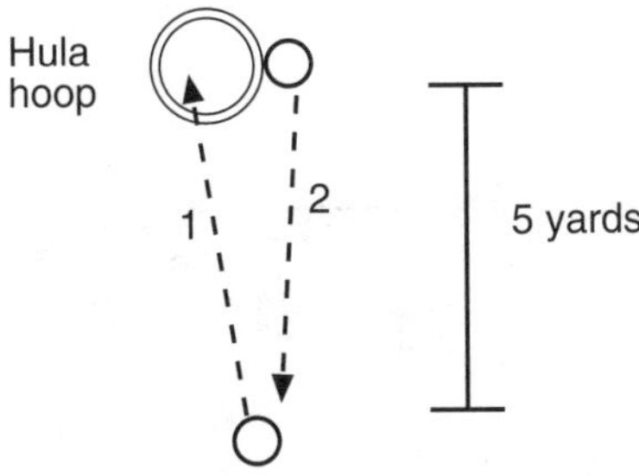

Repeat 5 times, then switch

"Keep a secure grip on the ball."
"Legs spread, weight on your back foot."
"Follow through."

Skill Practice 2 (10 minutes)

Divide players into groups of two. Give each pair a football. Instruct them to throw 10 balls to each other from a sitting position. This drill is used for developing arm strength, wrist snap, and accuracy. Start out at 5 yards apart and increase the distance as players become stronger.

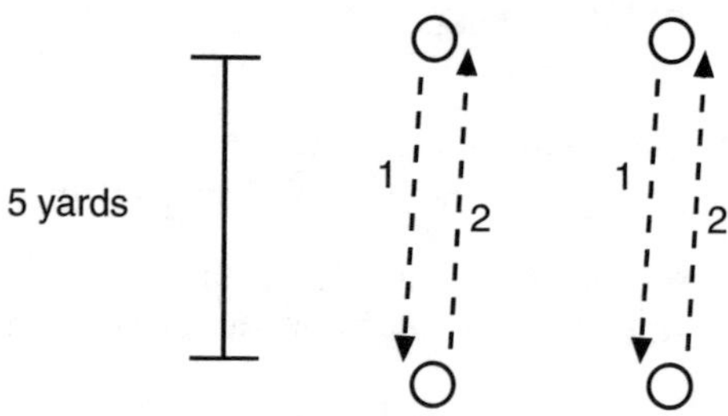

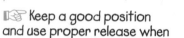

☞ Keep a good position and use proper release when throwing the football.

☞ Go over receiving rules (see page 131).

Game 2 (15 minutes)

Goal

Quarterbacks will hit their receivers with good passes.

Description

Divide the team into groups of three: a quarterback, a receiver, and a defensive back. The receiver runs three routes: one to the left, one to the right, and one down the middle; the quarterback attempts to complete all three passes. Then rotate players so that eventually everyone plays quarterback. For each pass completed, the quarterback and the receiver each receive one point.

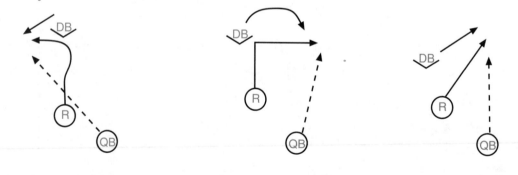

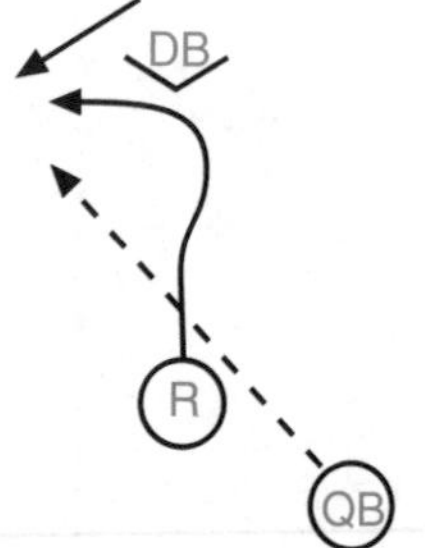

Play 1

Play 2

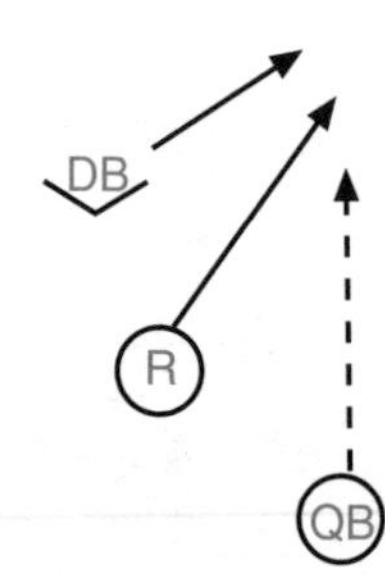

Play 3

Practice 2

Team Circle (5 minutes)

Key Idea: Responsibility

Gather the children into a group. "When you come to practice, you should be ready to do at least three things. Who can tell me what those things are?" Ask players to shout out their responses. Many responses might be appropriate, in addition to the three you are looking for. Acknowledge all good responses, and then say, "One: be ready to play. Two: learn new skills and work on 'old' skills. Three: work with others. When you do those three things, you have *fun*. Who wants to have fun?" Again ask them to shout out their responses. "Then the way to have fun is to be responsible to yourself and your teammates by doing those three things—by being ready to play, by working on skills, and by being good teammates."

Wrap-Up

Make summary comments about practice. Remind players of the next practice day and time.

Practice 3

PURPOSE

To learn a pass pattern

Equipment

One football for every two players (Nerf ball or youth-size: 10 1/4- to 10 1/2-inch)

Grass field 30 yards by 60 yards

Warm-Up (10 minutes)

Have the players run for 2 minutes and then lead them in stretches for their arms and legs. Conclude with a series of push-ups and jumping jacks.

Fitness Circle (5 minutes)

Key Idea: Cardiorespiratory health and fitness (moving your body)

Gather the children together. "Today I want to use a big word. It is *cardiorespiratory*. 'Cardio' means heart and 'respiratory' means lungs. Can you say the word? [Cardiorespiratory.] Cardiorespiratory exercises are those types that move most of your body for 15 minutes or longer without getting tired. Your breathing rate will increase and your heart will pump faster. Riding your bike, running, jumping rope, and playing tag are some exercises that are called cardiorespiratory exercises."

Activity: Yes, no, maybe so

"Put your thumb in the air if you think the statement I make is true. Point your thumb to the ground if you think the statement I make is false. If you are not sure, put one thumb in the air and the other thumb toward the ground."

1. "Running is a good cardiorespiratory exercise." After they vote ask, "Why?" [Yes, as long as it's not too fast.]
2. "Weight training is a good cardiorespiratory exercise." After they vote ask, "Why?" [No, it is a strength exercise.]
3. "Stretching is a good cardiorespiratory exercise." After they vote ask, "Why?" [No, it is a flexibility exercise.]

Game 1 (10 minutes)

Goal

Receivers will run routes and get open to receive passes.

Description

Split the players into four teams, two Team As and two Team Bs on two different parts of the field. Teams As begin and remain on offense for the first half of the game; Teams Bs are on offense for the second half of the game. The two Team As begin at midfield and move toward opposite goals. The defenses can play a zone (one player covers left, one middle, and one right) or player-to-player defense (with one player assigned to the quarterback). Receivers are to run however they want to in attempting to get open and receive a pass. Rotate offensive players to different positions after each play. Allow the receivers to run with the ball; the defenders must touch them with one hand to down them. Award one point for each pass caught.

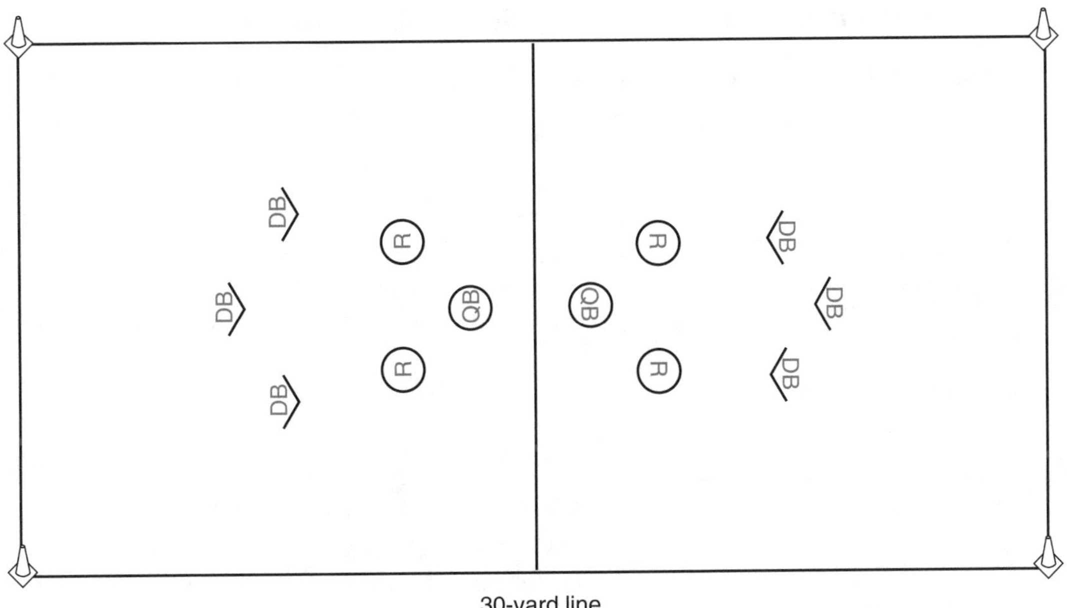

Coach: What were the receivers trying to do?
Players: Get open to catch passes.

Coach: How do you get open?
Players: By running to where the defender isn't, using different routes.

Coach: That's right. Let's learn one of those routes: the square-out.

Practice 3 (cont'd)

Skill Practice 1 (10 minutes)

1. Introduce, demonstrate, and explain how to catch the football on the run, using *the square-out pass pattern* (see page 117).
2. Have players practice catching the football using this pattern.

Description

Pair up players, with each pair having a ball. The pairs of players then throw each other passes using the square-out pass pattern.

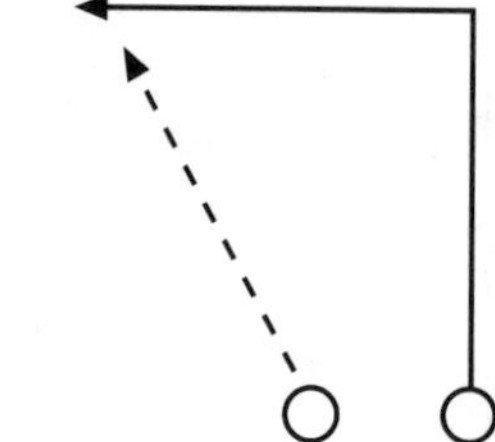

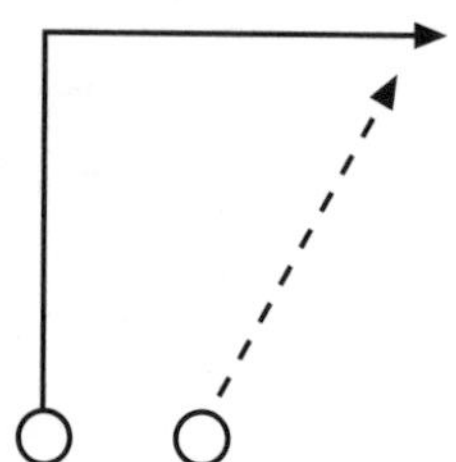

"Sharp cuts."

"Be soft all over."

"Look the ball into your hands."

"Catch the ball with your hands, not with your body."

Skill Practice 2 (10 minutes)

Show players the proper arm position for carrying the ball once they have caught a pass. Pair up players and give each pair a ball. The partners will rotate every play between receiver and quarterback. The receiver runs a square-out and receives a pass, then runs a few more yards, tucking the ball away properly. The receiver returns to the line of scrimmage, still using proper arm position. Then the players switch positions and repeat the drill.

Game 2 (10 minutes)

Goal

Players will catch the ball while running square-out pass patterns.

Description

Repeat game 1, with the receivers running square-outs.

Practice 3

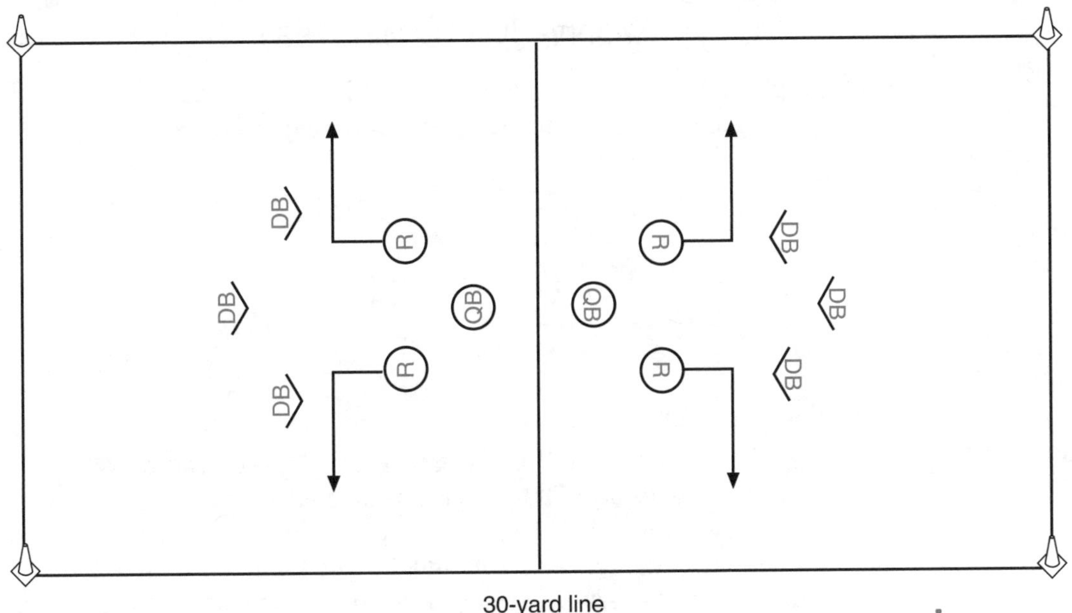

30-yard line

Variation

Make the games and skill practices easier or harder for the kids by adjusting the length of the patterns.

☞ Being a good receiver involves more than speed.

☞ Go over the no-block rule (see page 132).

Team Circle (5 minutes)

Key Idea: Responsibility

Gather the children into a circle. Stand in the middle of the circle with a ball. "I'm going to show you two different ways to handle the same situation. Think about which is the best way to handle this." Choose a player to receive a pass from you. Make a bad pass and then stomp angrily away from the group. Retrieve the ball and make another bad pass. This time run to get the ball and make a pass that goes directly to the player. "If you think the first response is the way to handle making a bad pass, stand to my left. If you think the second way is better, stand to my right." Ask players to explain their choices. "It's important to be a good sport in flag football." Highlight how and why. "That's being responsible to your teammates."

Wrap-Up

Make summary comments about practice. Remind players of the next practice day and time.

Practice 4

☞ PURPOSE

To learn two new pass patterns

Equipment

- One football for every two players (Nerf ball or youth-size: 10 1/4- to 10 1/2-inch)
- Grass field 30 yards by 60 yards

Warm-Up (10 minutes)

Have the players jog one lap around the field and then lead them in jumping jacks and stretches for their arms and legs.

Fitness Circle (5 minutes)

Key Idea: Muscle fitness

Gather the children together. "Muscle strength tells you how strong your muscles are. That is, muscle strength shows you how much your muscles can lift. Muscle strength is improved by making your muscles work harder—a lot harder. To get stronger, muscles need to be exercised every other day. The exercises must be hard enough that the muscles get tired after doing the exercise three to ten times. Some of the better exercises for getting stronger are those that you can do with weights. How many of you have seen someone lift weights? How many of you have tried lifting weights? How did it feel? If you don't have weights, you can use your body as weight."

Activity: Three exercises

"You need to be strong to play football. In addition to strong leg muscles, you need arm and abdominal (belly) muscles that will help you do your best. There are three 'harder type' exercises that will help your muscles get stronger—push-ups, partner pull-ups, and abdominal curls."

Practice 4

Game 1 (10 minutes)

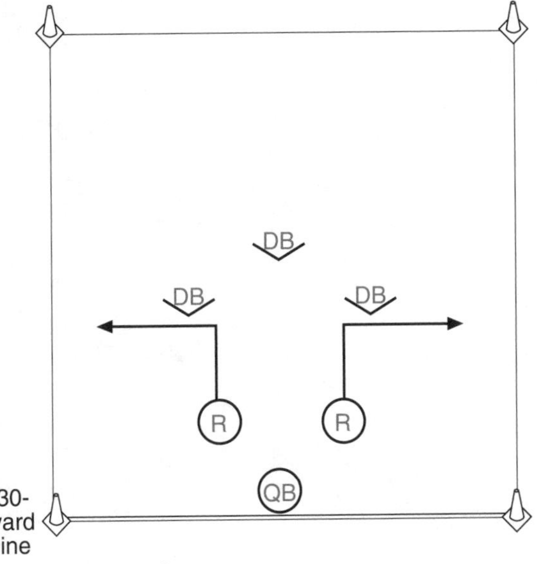

Goal

Receivers will run square-out patterns, catch passes, and score touchdowns.

Description

Play games of 3 v 3. Have receivers run square-outs. The offense starts 30 yards away from the goal and has five passes to attempt to score. Play a zone or player-to-player defense. Each completion is worth one point; a touchdown is worth six. Switch offense and defense after a touchdown or after five passes, whichever comes first. The offense always begins 30 yards from the goal. The defense has to down the ball by touching the ball carrier with one hand.

Coach: What was the goal of the game?
Players: To get open, catch passes, and score.

Coach: How can you get open?
Players: By running square-out patterns.

Coach: That's right. And two other ways are to run curl and slant patterns.

Skill Practice 1 (10 minutes)

1. Introduce, demonstrate, and explain how to catch the football on the run, using the *curl pass pattern* (see page 117).
2. Have players practice catching the football using the curl pass pattern.

Description

Divide players into pairs, each pair with one football. One player runs a curl pattern while his or her partner throws a pass. Have receivers run five curls, then switch roles so that their partners can run curls.

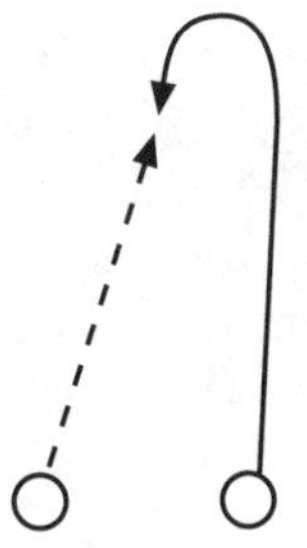

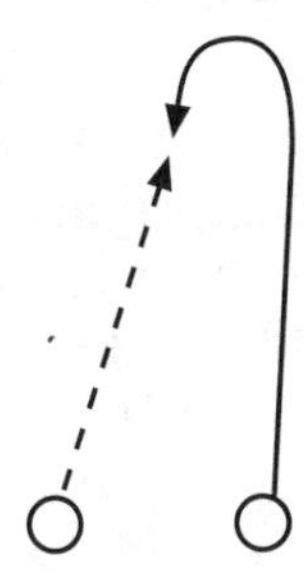

Practice 4 (cont'd)

"Curl back!"
"Proper hand position."
"Tuck the ball away."

Practice 2 (10 minutes)

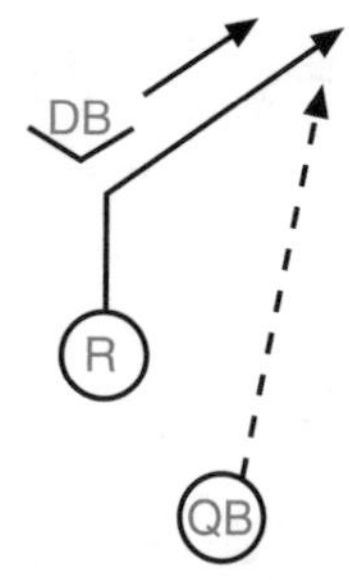

Practice, demonstrate, and explain the *slant pattern* (see page 117). Have players practice running the slant pattern.

Description

Split your squad into three-player groups. In each group, there's a quarterback, a receiver, and a defensive back. The receivers run slant patterns and attempt to catch passes. Rotate positions after a receiver has run the route three times.

"Change your speed."
"Change your direction."
"Make sharp cuts."

Game 2 (10 minutes)

Goal

Players will catch the ball while running the correct pass pattern.

Description

Divide the players into four groups of three kids each and set each group on a quadrant of the field. Designate a quarterback and two receivers for each team. Each team will begin at midfield and will proceed down the field, trying to score. The ball is down where it is caught. You call out the pass patterns for the receivers to execute. If a team scores a touchdown, they begin again at midfield. The team that advances the most down the field or scores the most touchdowns is the winner.

Practice 4

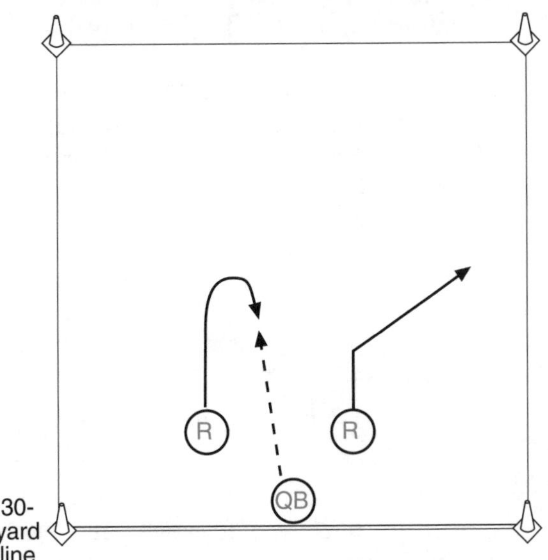

☞ Look the ball into your hands.

☞ Go over defensive rules (see page 132).

Team Circle (5 minutes)

Key Idea: Honesty

Gather the children into a group. "What is an offsides violation?" Listen to their responses. Choose a player to help demonstrate responses. "Should you admit to a violation if no official sees it? Those who think yes, stand to my right. Those who think no, stand to my left." Wait for children to choose. "When you know you've been offsides or committed another violation, you should raise your hand. You should never take unfair advantage of other players. Can you think of other ways honesty is practiced on the field?" Listen to responses and discuss. "All those show honesty."

Wrap-Up

Make summary comments about practice. Remind players of the next practice day and time.

Practice 5

PURPOSE

To stop offensive progress

Equipment

- One football for every two players (Nerf ball or youth-size: 10 1/4- to 10 1/2-inch)
- 12 towels or cones to mark zones
- Flag belts for all players

Warm-Up (10 minutes)

Have the players jog around the field and then come back and run pass patterns. Put defensive backs on each receiver so that it puts pressure on the receiver and the quarterbacks throwing. Have two lines going with two quarterbacks throwing.

Fitness Circle (5 minutes)

Key Idea: Muscle fitness

Gather the children together. "To move your body, you need muscles and joints. What is a joint?" [A joint is where two bones are placed close together and allow you to move.] "Let me use my knee as an example of a joint. There is a bone in my upper leg and two bones in my lower leg. When the muscles in the back of my leg contract, they pull on my bones to make my lower leg move backward. When the muscles on the front of my leg contract, they move my leg forward.

"If I want good flexibility, I need to make sure that my muscles contract and extend properly. If they do, I am said to have good flexibility. Good flexibility helps prevent injuries and helps you play your sport better. The quadriceps stretch and modified hamstring stretch are two good leg flexibility exercises for you to learn."

Game 1 (10 minutes)

Goal

Defenders will stop the offense from scoring by pulling the ball carrier's flag.

Description

Play two 3 v 3 games, with each offense beginning at midfield and going toward opposite end zones. The defense plays "cold," allowing a receiver to catch the ball, but then immediately tries to pull the flag. (The defense can play zone or player-to-player.) The receivers do not go farther than 5 yards beyond the line of scrimmage to catch the ball. The offense goes for five plays or until they score a touchdown, whichever comes first; then the defense and offense switch sides. Award the defense one point for not allowing the ball carrier to advance more than 5 yards beyond the point of reception and six points for not allowing a touchdown.

Coach: What was the goal of the game?
Players: To pull the flag.

Coach: What's the best way to pull the flag?
Players: Try to grab it.

Coach: Should you lunge for the runner or let the runner come to you?
Players: Wait for the runner to come to you.

Coach: Should you keep your weight back, on the balls of your feet (indicate what these are), or should you get up on your toes?
Players: Keep your weight on the balls of your feet.

Coach: Good. Let's practice pulling flags.

Skill Practice 1 (10 minutes)

1. Practice, demonstrate, and explain how to *pull the flag* (see page 123).
2. Have players practice pulling flags.

Description

Mark two zones, each 3 yards wide by 3 yards long, with cones or towels. Assign six players (three on offense, three on defense) to each zone. The offensive and defensive players line up single file; this is a one-on-one drill. The first two players in the offensive line each have a football. The first player runs through the zone, attempting to elude the defender, who tries to pull his or her flag. After the play, the ball carrier tosses the ball to the second offensive player in line as the next set of players get ready to go. (In this way the players never have to wait, because the next offensive player will always have a ball and be ready to go immediately after the preceding play is over.) The ball carrier then goes to the end of the defensive line, and the defender who just pulled the flag goes to the end of the offensive line.

"Use the wraparound method."
"Keep your eye on the target."
"Soft hands."

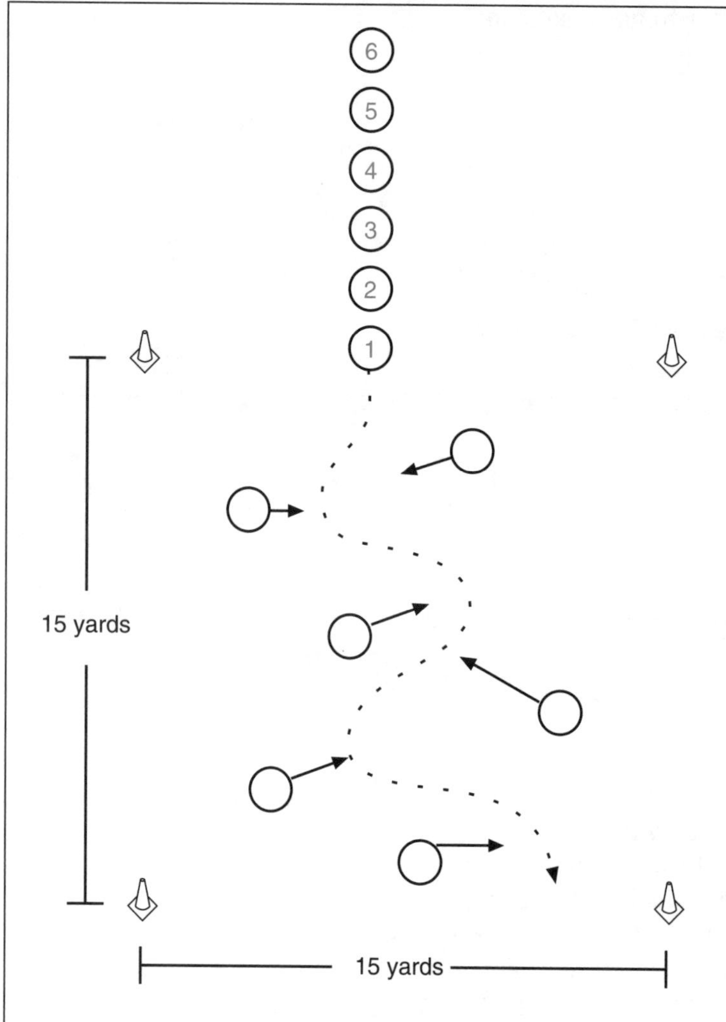

Skill Practice 2 (10 minutes)

Mark a 15-yard by 15-yard zone with towels or cones. Assign half your players to offense, and half to defense. Give each offensive player a ball. They stand in line outside the zone; the defenders arrange themselves in random order within the zone, about 3 to 5 yards apart. Ball carriers try to run through the maze one at a time. The defenders can't swarm on the ball carrier; this is a multiple one-on-one exercise in which only the closest defender can attempt to pull the flag.

The ball carrier continues through the maze until his or her flag is pulled. When that happens, the ball carrier becomes a defender in the zone and the player who pulled the flag takes the ball and goes to the offensive line. (If the flag isn't pulled, the offensive player remains on offense.)

Game 2 (10 minutes)

Goal

Defenders will pull flags under game-like situations.

Description

Play two 3 v 3 games, with each offense beginning at midfield and going toward opposite end zones. Each offense has five plays in which to score a touchdown; after a score or after five plays, the offense and defense switch sides. The defense can play zone or player-to-player. Give the defense one point for each flag pulled and six points when they don't allow a touchdown within the five plays.

Variations

To make game 2 easier, play 3 v 4 or 3 v 5, rotating players in after each play. To make it harder, play 4 v 3.

☞ Let the offensive player come to you—don't lunge and get faked out.

☞ Go over the flag-guarding rule (see page 133).

Practice 5

Team Circle
(5 minutes)

Key Idea: Responsibility

Gather the children into a circle. "I want everyone to run in a circle following the person in front of you without bumping into each other. Keep a space about as long as a bicycle between you, and don't go ahead of the person in front of you." Encourage children to run slow enough to follow all the directions. Continue the activity for 1 minute. "Everyone stop. Did you bump into each other? Did anyone get upset with the person in front of you? You kept your body under control by not going ahead of the person in front of you. You kept your emotions under control by not getting upset with the person ahead of you—they couldn't move any faster since you were all running in a circle as a group. Everyone can stay safe and learn when everyone is responsible for themselves."

Wrap-Up

Make summary comments about practice. Remind players of the next practice day and time.

Practice 6

☞ PURPOSE

To learn a new pass pattern

Equipment

- One football for every two players (Nerf ball or youth-size: 10 1/4- to 10 1/2-inch)
- Grass field 30 yards by 60 yards
- Flag belts for all players

Warm-Up (10 minutes)

Have the players jog one lap around the field and then lead them in jumping jacks and stretches for their arms and legs. Choose two quarterbacks to throw to receivers running the pass patterns learned earlier (square-outs, curls, slants).

Fitness Circle (5 minutes)

Key Idea: Body type

Gather the children together. "Football players come in all shapes and sizes. Some are short, some are tall, some are heavy, and some are thin. Doctors say there are three body types—heavy, muscular, and thin. With children your age, there are usually only two—thin and heavy. As you grow older, each of you will become similar to one of the three body types.

"People with different body types do better at different sports and activities. The heavier player may do well in football since his size helps him block or tackle. Thin people may do well at things like running and bicycling. The muscular person might also excel at boxing, weight lifting, or wrestling. Each body type is important, and you should be proud of the body you have and of what it can do."

Game 1 (10 minutes)

Goal

Receivers will run routes against defenders and get open to receive passes.

Description

Play 4 v 4; have one quarterback and three receivers on offense and four defenders on defense, playing either a zone or player-to-player. After every three plays, the team on defense goes to offense, the team on offense goes to the sideline, and the team on the sideline goes to defense. The offense runs "hot" (full speed); the defense runs "cold"

Practice 6

(half speed), allowing the offense to catch the ball when patterns are run correctly and then pulling the flag. Encourage receivers to run the patterns they've learned—square-outs, curls, and slants—but they can run whatever way they want to in attempting to get open and receive passes. Count one point for each pass caught.

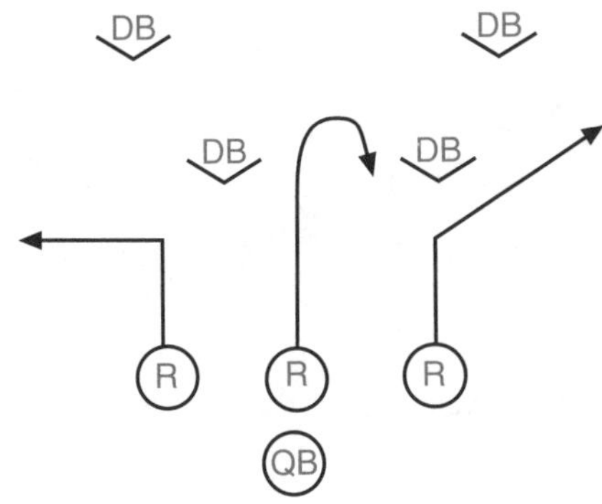

Coach: What was the goal of the game?
Players: To get open and catch passes.

Coach: Why is it so important to run a certain route?
Players: So the quarterback knows where to throw the ball.

Coach: What are the routes you've already learned?
Players: Square-outs, curls, slants.

Coach: Let's learn a new route.

Skill Practice (15 minutes)

1. Introduce, demonstrate, and explain the *streak pass pattern* (see page 117).
2. Have players practice running this route.

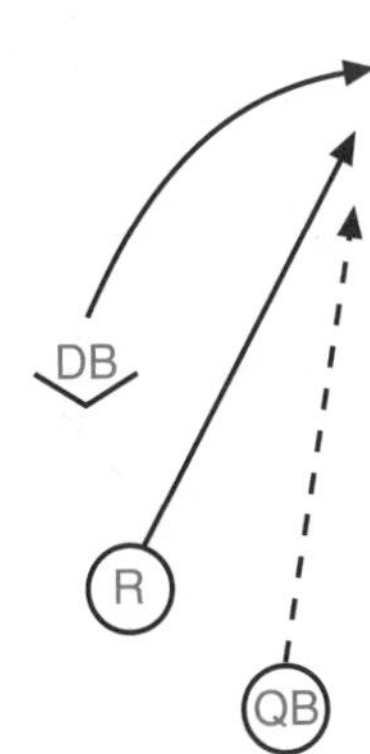

Description

Split your squad into three-player groups. In each group, there's a quarterback, a receiver, and a defensive back. The same receiver runs the streak route and attempts to catch a pass. Rotate positions after a receiver has run the route three times.

"Change your speed."
"Watch the ball into your hands."

Game 2 (15 minutes)

Goal

Receivers will run various pass patterns, move the ball downfield, and score.

Description

Split your squad into two teams. Each team plays this game separately on one half of the field. Each team is on offense; there is no defense. Each team begins at midfield and works its way downfield by completing passes. The ball is down where caught. Tell wide receivers (the ones on either side of the ball, farthest from the ball) to run square-outs; the others can run either a curl, streak, or slant. Award one point for each completed pass and two points for each touchdown. A touchdown only counts if at least three different receivers have caught the ball. After a touchdown, rotate players so that someone else plays quarterback.

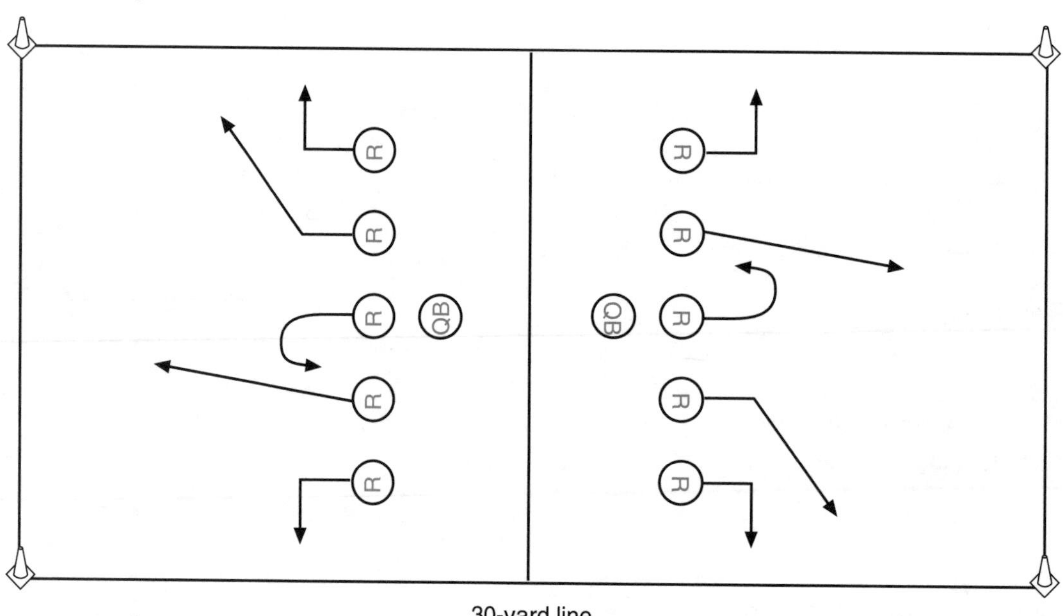

Practice 6

Variation

Make game 2 harder by playing defense.

Team Circle (5 minutes)

Key Idea: Responsibility

Gather the children into a group. Choose two players to help role play. Set up a triangle of you and the two players. Let the children know you're role playing with them. All three take turns passing. When it's your turn, miss the pass and role play yourself as a player: "I couldn't get that pass! It was your fault—you made a bad pass!" Now as coach: "I want you to think about players who make excuses and blame others for their mistakes. Stand to my left if you think it's OK to make excuses when you make mistakes. Stand to my right if you think you should try to learn and work harder to improve." Ask players about their choices. "Not making excuses is taking responsibility for yourself."

Wrap-Up

Make summary comments about practice. Remind players of the next practice day and time.

☞ Learn to find the open space on the field.

☞ Go over running rules (see page 131).

Practice 7

PURPOSE

To run effective pass patterns and get open

Equipment

- One football for every two players (Nerf ball or youth-size: 10 1/4- to 10 1/2-inch)
- Grass field 30 yards by 60 yards
- Flag belts for all players

Warm-Up (10 minutes)

Have the players jog for 2 minutes and then lead them in stretches. Have kids throw passes to each other taking turns being quarterback and going out for passes as a receiver.

Fitness Circle (5 minutes)

Key Idea: Training and conditioning

Gather the children together. "There are two important things to remember when playing sports such as flag football. You need to warm up and cool down properly. Today we'll talk about the warm-up. The warm-up prepares your muscles and helps get your heart ready for more vigorous exercise. The best warm-up exercises are walking, slow jogging, range-of-motion exercises like arm circles, and stretching exercises like the quad stretch. Usually, you should warm up for 5 to 10 minutes before playing a game."

Activity: Warm-up for flag football

Do the warm-up exercises found in chapter 10. "Let's try a sample warm-up for flag football. Now you are ready to play!"

Game 1 (15 minutes)

Goal

Players will run routes that will get them open.

Description

Play two simultaneous 3 v 3 games. Have receivers run various routes against defenders, with you telling the offense (so that the defense doesn't hear) the routes. The defense plays zone or player-to-player and must pull the flag. The offense gets six plays; then offense and defense switch sides. Give one point for each catch and an additional point if the catch was made while the receiver was running the correct route.

Practice 7

Coach: What was the goal of the game?
Players: To run routes and get open to catch passes.

Coach: Why is it so important to run sharp cuts and make your fakes believable when running pass patterns?
Players: You take fewer steps when you run sharp cuts. Making your fakes believable will help you get open.

Skill Practice (15 minutes)

Split your squad into three-player groups. In each group there's a quarterback, a receiver, and a defensive back. The same receiver runs a curl, a square-out, and a slant, and attempts to catch passes. Rotate positions after a receiver has run the three patterns.

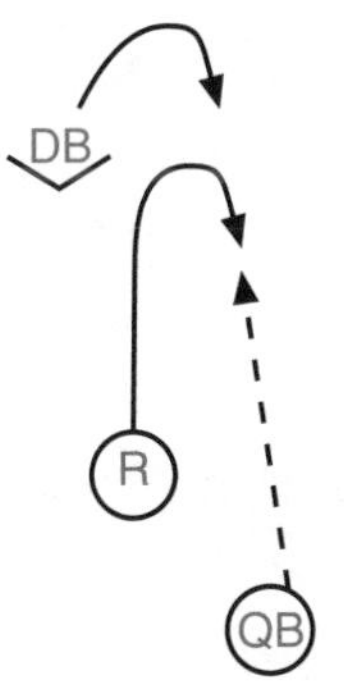

Play 1

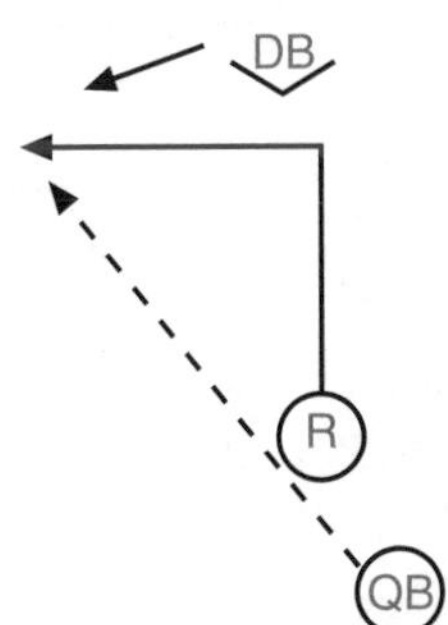

Play 2

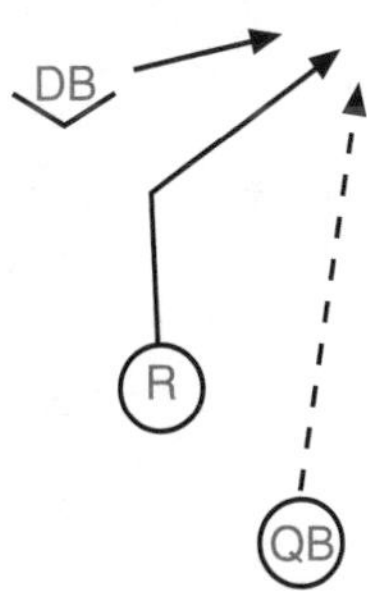

Play 3

"Make good fakes!"
"Run an exact pattern."

☞ Playing smart is a large part of being a good pass receiver.

☞ Go over the offsides rule (see page 132).

Game 2 (10 minutes)

Goal

Players will catch the football in an open position on the field.

Description

Play two simultaneous 3 v 3 games. The two teams on offense run a 2-minute drill and see how many completions they can make in that time limit. The receivers run any of the patterns they have learned (square-out, curl, slant, or streak). The defense plays zone or player-to-player and must pull the flag. Then switch offenses and defenses and repeat. Do this twice, and give one point for each completion in the time limit.

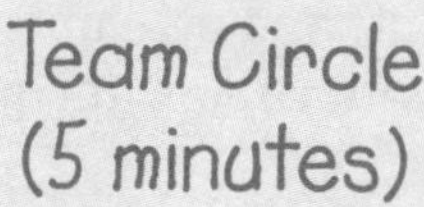

Team Circle (5 minutes)

Key Idea: Caring

Gather the children into a circle. Stand in the middle of the circle with a ball. Choose two children to pass the ball with you. "We're going to work on our passing skills." Pass repeatedly to them but not to the others. "Tell me how you felt to have only two players get the passes?" Listen to their responses. "Sharing the ball with your teammates shows you care about them. What other things can you do to show you care about your teammates?" Their responses should include encouragement, positive comments for good play, forgiving players that make mistakes, and so on. "Good. Those are all ways you can show you care."

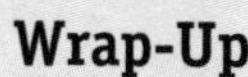

Wrap-Up

Make summary comments about practice. Remind players of the next practice day and time.

Practice 8

Warm-Up (5 minutes)

Have the players jog for 3 minutes and then lead them in stretches.

Fitness Circle (5 minutes)

Key Idea: Training and conditioning

Gather the children together. "Last time you learned about the warm-up. Today we will learn about the cool-down. The cool-down's job is to return your heart rate to a lower level, prevent muscle soreness, improve flexibility, and reduce tension through relaxation exercises. Think of the cool-down as a warm-up in reverse. At the end of the practice, we'll do a cool-down to finish up."

Game 1 (15 minutes)

Goal

Receivers will run good pass routes and score touchdowns.

Description

Play two simultaneous 3 v 3 games on separate halves of the field. Have receivers run various routes against defenders, with you and an assistant telling the two offenses (so that the defense doesn't hear) the routes. The defense plays zone or player-to-player and must pull the flag. The offense gets five plays to score; then offense and defense switch. Give two points per catch *only* if the route was run correctly, and six points for a touchdown.

Coach: What was the goal of the game?
Players: To run good routes and score touchdowns.

Coach: How important is it to run the correct route?
Players: Very important, because the quarterback must know where everyone is on the field to be able to complete the pass.

Coach: We've learned curls, square-outs, slants, and streaks. What's another way you can get open?
Players: Run a different pattern.

PURPOSE

To learn a new pass pattern

Equipment

- One football for every two players (Nerf ball or youth-size: 10 1/4- to 10 1/2-inch)
- Grass field 30 yards by 60 yards
- Flag belts for all players

Practice 8 (cont'd)

Skill Practice (10 minutes)

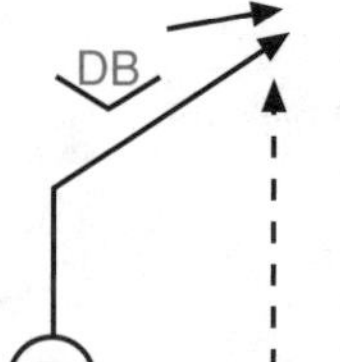

1. Introduce, demonstrate, and explain how to run the *post pattern* (see page 117).
2. Have players practice running post patterns.

Description

Split your squad into three-player groups. In each group, there's a quarterback, a receiver, and a defensive back. The receivers run post patterns and attempt to catch passes. Rotate positions after a receiver has run the route three times.

"Make cuts believable."
"Run your route!"

☞ Everyone must know the routes and run them precisely so that the quarterback can find and throw to an open receiver.

☞ Go over the illegal rushing rule (see page 132).

Game 2 (20 minutes)

Goal

Players will run routes correctly and score touchdowns.

Description

Repeat game 1.

Practice 8

Team Circle (5 minutes)

Key Idea: Respect

Gather the children into a group. "I'm going to ask you some questions about things I notice on this team. Tell me if you agree. Do you try to learn new skills at practice? Do you work hard to improve your skills? Do you help your teammates? Do you follow directions? Do you feel good about yourselves when you play well?" Listen to responses following each question. "Think about the teammates you play against in games at practice. It's important to think of your teammates in the same way you think of yourself. You respect yourself, and you should respect your teammates. They are a lot like you and are learning the same things."

Wrap-Up

Make summary comments about practice. Remind players of the next practice day and time.

Practice 9

☞ **PURPOSE**

To run effective pass patterns and get open

Equipment

- One football for every two players (Nerf ball or youth-size: 10 1/4- to 10 1/2-inch)
- Grass field 30 yards by 60 yards
- Flag belts for all players

Warm-Up (5 minutes)

Have the players jog one lap around the field and then pair up to throw to each other, running the pass patterns they have learned.

Fitness Circle (5 minutes)

Key Idea: Healthy habits

Gather the children together. "Young people drink lots of different beverages such as soda pop, water, fruit juices, fruit drinks, and milk. Some of these beverages are better for you than others. Milk contains protein and lots of vitamins and minerals. Fruit drinks usually contain quite a bit of sugar and do not have much in the way of vitamins. Some do have vitamin C added. Fruit juices, like fruit drinks, can have lots of sugar, but they contain vitamins and minerals. Soda pop, on the other hand, is loaded with sugar (unless diet) and has no protein, vitamins, or minerals. Water is great for replacing liquids lost during practice."

Activity: Choosing the best beverages

"Can you rank the following beverages according to nutritional value?"

Water (unique)
Milk (1)
Fruit juice (2)
Fruit drink (3)
Soda pop (4)

Game 1 (15 minutes)

Goal

Players will use the routes they have learned to catch passes and score touchdowns.

Description

Play 6 v 6. Have receivers run various routes against defenders, with you telling the offense (so that the defense doesn't hear) the routes. Have the defense play player-to-player. They must pull the flag to down the ball carrier. The offense gets five plays to score; then offense and defense switch. Give two points per catch *only* if the route was run correctly, and six points for a touchdown.

Practice 9

Coach: What was the goal of the game?
Players: To run correct pass routes and score touchdowns.

Coach: Why is it important to run the correct route?
Players: Because the quarterback must know where everyone is on the field to be able to complete the pass.

Skill Practice (15 minutes)

Put the kids into groups of four (a quarterback and three receivers). The receivers will line up and run a route, one at a time. You call the pass pattern for each receiver, varying it from receiver to receiver. Make sure the quarterback also rotates to being a receiver.

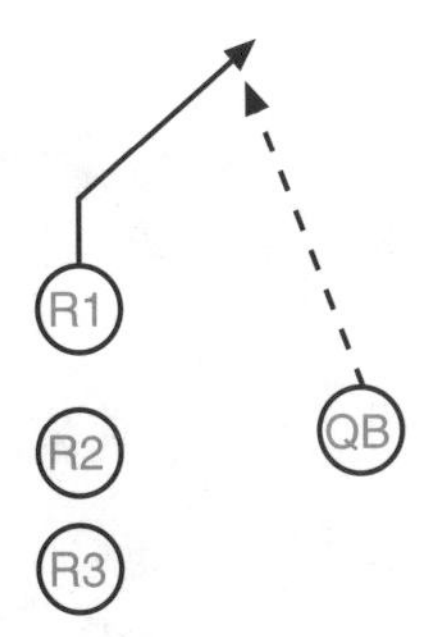

"Run your route!"

Game 2 (15 minutes)

Goal

Players will correctly run routes with pressure on the quarterback.

Description

Play 6 v 6. You call out the routes for the receivers, and the quarterback throws to one of the receivers (let only the offense know the routes, or instruct the defense to play a "cold" defense). Have the defense play player-to-player. They must pull the flag to down the ball carrier. A rusher puts pressure on the quarterback after 5 seconds, counted out by you or your assistant. Give a point for each catch made off of a pattern that is run correctly, and six points for a touchdown scored in five plays or less. Rotate offense and defense after a touchdown or after five plays, whichever occurs first.

☞ Running correct routes will spread the field and make it easy for the quarterback to find the open receiver.

☞ Go over the defensive holding rule (see page 132).

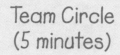

Team Circle (5 minutes)

Key Idea: Caring

Gather the children into a group near midfield. Have a ball ready. Ask a child in the group to pass to you. Make a bad pass. "That pass wasn't very good, was it? That was a mistake. What should you say to your teammates when they make mistakes?" Listen to their responses. "What could you say to make your teammate feel better? What could you say to make him feel worse?" Listen to their responses. Have players change the negative comments to positive ones. "It's very important to forgive mistakes and to be understanding of others, just as you would want them to be of you. Making mistakes is part of learning. Saying something that makes your teammates feel better shows you care about them."

Wrap-Up

Make summary comments about practice. Remind players of the next practice day and time.

Practice 10

Warm-Up (5 minutes)

Have the players jog one lap around the field and then pair up to throw to each other, running the pass patterns they have learned.

Fitness Circle (5 minutes)

Key Idea: Healthy habits

Gather the children together. "Seven out of ten high school students have tried smoking, and one out of four young people smoke before the age of thirteen! Many young people try smoking because they want to be part of the gang or prove that they are cool or big (older). Besides causing lots of diseases, smoking also 'cuts people's wind.' That means when you play a sport such as football, you can't get your breath as well as a person who doesn't smoke.

"Once a person starts smoking it is hard to stop. Doctors use the word *addiction* to describe what it means when a person can't stop using cigarettes. They 'need' the cigarette to calm down or to 'pick themselves up.'"

Activity: Voting

"I am going to read a statement to you. If you agree, put your thumb in the air. If you disagree, put your thumb down. If you don't know, put your arms across your chest.

1. How many of you think smoking causes heart attacks?
2. How many of you think smoking makes exercise harder?
3. How many of you worry because your parents, grandparents, brothers, or sisters smoke?
4. How many of you think it's okay for doctors to smoke?
5. How many of you think smoking is okay?"

PURPOSE

To cover pass receivers

Equipment

- One football for every two players (Nerf ball or youth-size: 10 1/4- to 10 1/2-inch)
- Grass field 30 yards by 60 yards
- Flag belts for all players

Game 1 (10 minutes)

Goal

Defenders will cover pass receivers to prevent them from catching passes and advancing the ball.

Description

Play 6 v 6, with the offense beginning at midfield. On defense, play player-to-player and have a rusher put light pressure on the quarterback (that is, not downing the quarterback, but putting pressure on him or her). The defense must pull the flag to down the ball carrier. Give the offense two points for every completed pass and six points if they score a touchdown in five plays or less. The defense will receive one point for every incomplete pass that the defense doesn't touch, two points for an incomplete pass that is tipped or touched by the defense, three points for an interception, and six points for not allowing a touchdown. After five plays or after a touchdown (whichever comes first), switch offense and defense.

Coach: What was the goal of the game?
Players: To prevent receivers from catching the ball or from advancing the ball if they do catch it.

Coach: When should a defensive back look for the ball?
Players: When the receiver looks for it.

Skill Practice 1 (10 minutes)

1. Introduce, demonstrate, and explain how to *cover receivers* (see pages 124-125).
2. Have your players practice covering receivers.

Description

Line players up and stand in front of them holding the football. Point to different directions on the field (back, forward, right, and left) and have the kids run with the proper footwork as they change direction.

"Fast footwork."
"Drop step at the start."

Practice 10

Skill Practice 2 (10 minutes)

Divide the players into two groups. Each group has a quarterback and two or three receivers as well as two or three defensive backs. The receivers will take turns going one-on-one against the defensive backs, who will practice proper coverage. Call out pass routes for each receiver and help the defenders line up at the proper distance.

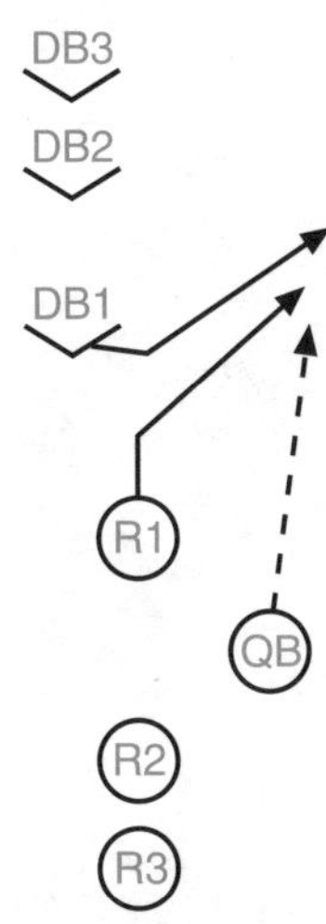

"Stick with the receiver!"
"Look for the ball when the receiver looks for the ball."

Game 2 (15 minutes)

Goal

Defenders will stop the pass.

Description

Repeat game 1.

☞ Always keep the offensive receiver in front of you. Never turn your back on the receiver.

☞ Go over the pass interference rule (see page 132).

Team Circle
(5 minutes)

Key Idea: Respect

Gather the children into a group. "What have you learned about flag football this season?" Listen to their responses. "What does respect have to do with playing flag football or any sport? It takes many years to master the game of flag football, so flag football deserves your respect. Every year there are new skills to learn and improve on; every year you play you'll get better. That's why you need to come back next year! What examples of players showing respect have you seen this flag football season?" Listen to their responses and discuss.

Wrap-Up

Make summary comments about what everyone learned over the season. Encourage players to come back next year.

Part III

The Building Blocks

In part II we provided you with the plans for coaching flag football, starting with the season plans for teaching 4- through 7-year-olds the basics of flag football. We presented important fitness and character development concepts, then gave detailed plans for conducting each practice session. In part III we'll present more information about how to teach the subject matter planned in part II. In chapter 8 we'll review teaching basic flag football tactics and skills, and in chapter 9 we'll examine the rules of the game, along with a few unwritten traditions that are useful to know. In chapter 10 we'll tell you more about the basic fitness and safety concepts we want you to integrate into your flag football teaching, and in chapter 11 we'll do the same for teaching character development.

The more you understand the subject matter you teach, the better you're likely to teach it. See the information here as a good starting point, but feel free to learn more by exploring resources listed in appendix A at the end of this book.

chapter

8

Teaching Flag Football Tactics and Skills

This is where we'll give you in-depth information about the tactics and skills you'll be teaching to your YMCA Rookies players. We'll start with team tactics, then move to individual skills. Much of the information here—especially in the tactics sections—is geared to preparing players for competition against other teams. Remember, in YMCA Rookies you won't be competing against other teams, but the tactical information will be helpful for you as you hone your players' skills and knowledge of how to respond in various game situations. When they move on to YMCA Winners, they will be putting the tactics to fuller use. Please read the tactics sections with this in mind.

Remember to use the IDEA approach to teaching skills—introduce, demonstrate, and explain the skill, and attend to players as they practice the skill. If you aren't familiar with flag football skills, rent or buy a video to see the skills performed or find a book on flag football skills (see appendix A for suggested additional resources).

With young, inexperienced players you'll have your work cut out for you. Emphasize proper mechanics, rather than outcomes, to give players a solid foundation to build on.

Offensive Tactics

The objectives you set must be realistic and important—not only to you, but also to your players. If your team is incapable of reaching the goals, or is not interested in achieving them, then they serve little purpose.

Scoring is the obvious objective when a flag football team is on offense. But scoring is an outcome produced by the team's ability to

- execute consistently,
- move the football, and
- maintain possession.

To execute, move the ball, and maintain possession at the YMCA Rookies level, you have to have a strong passing game. We'll look at the passing game after we explore the first three tactics.

Execute Consistently

Consistent execution comes from consistent practice. For your players to execute consistently, they need many repetitions of the tactics and skills that they are learning. If your players know that a team goal is consistent execution, they'll be more eager to perform the skills as they continue to learn the fundamentals.

Teach your receivers the proper patterns to run and your quarterbacks the proper depth to drop to throw the football. Your players need to practice running a pattern many times before they'll feel confident that it will work.

By giving the players enough repetitions to eliminate mistakes, you'll help your team execute consistently.

Move the Football

The object on offense is to move down the field and score by using good passing plays. The offense must believe they can march the football down the field regardless of who they're playing or the defense they're facing. Select pass patterns and plays that use the strengths of your offense.

Maintain Possession

Obviously, when the offense controls the football, the opponent cannot score. To keep control, the offense must consistently produce first downs. An offensive game of short, quick passes is hard to stop. Maintaining possession is especially important when your offense has a narrow lead at the end of a game.

Passing Game

At this level, running plays are not allowed. The offense *must* use forward passes to move the ball downfield (of course, receivers can run with the ball once they catch it). The forward pass is a potent way to gain yardage and score points. Throwing the football helps develop individual players, forces the defense to defend the whole field, and gains yardage on offense.

You must do a good job of preparing the quarterbacks and receivers in the basic skills covered later in this chapter. Keep the passing attack simple so that the quarterbacks and receivers know what to do. Timing is important to the success of a passing attack, so allow time for players to perform many repetitions of the basic patterns.

The passing game starts with a pass tree (see figure 8.1). These are patterns that we recommend YMCA Rookies receivers run to get open to catch the football. The quarterback drops straight back and throws the football to the open receiver.

Different pass patterns may be helpful in different situations. Here are the five pass patterns we recommend you teach your YMCA Rookies players.

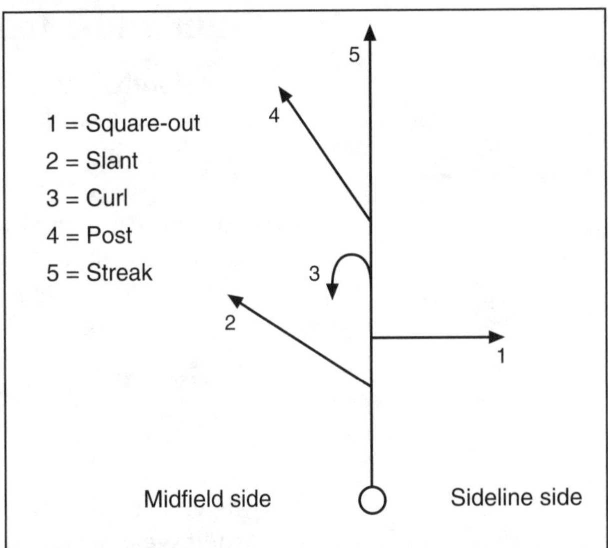

Figure 8.1 Pass tree.

- **Curl**—When the defensive player retreats too fast, use the curl pattern. The receiver drives deep and then curls back to the football (see figure 8.2a).
- **Square-out**—The square-out pattern is very successful when the defensive player is playing off the receiver (see figure 8.2b). The receiver runs downfield 5 to 10 yards and then cuts sharply to the sideline, catching the ball just before stepping out of bounds.
- **Slant**—The slant is similar to a square-out, but the cut is not as sharp (see figure 8.2c). With this pattern you can often gain more yardage than with a square-out, though it can be a more difficult (longer) pass for a quarterback to throw.
- **Streak**—Use the streak if the defensive back is playing tight on a receiver with speed. The receiver shows a curl move then breaks to the outside and sprints downfield (see figure 8.2d).
- **Post**—The post is similar to the streak, but the receiver breaks to one side and heads long (see figure 8.2e).

The passing game takes time to develop, and you must be patient to bring the separate parts of this offense together.

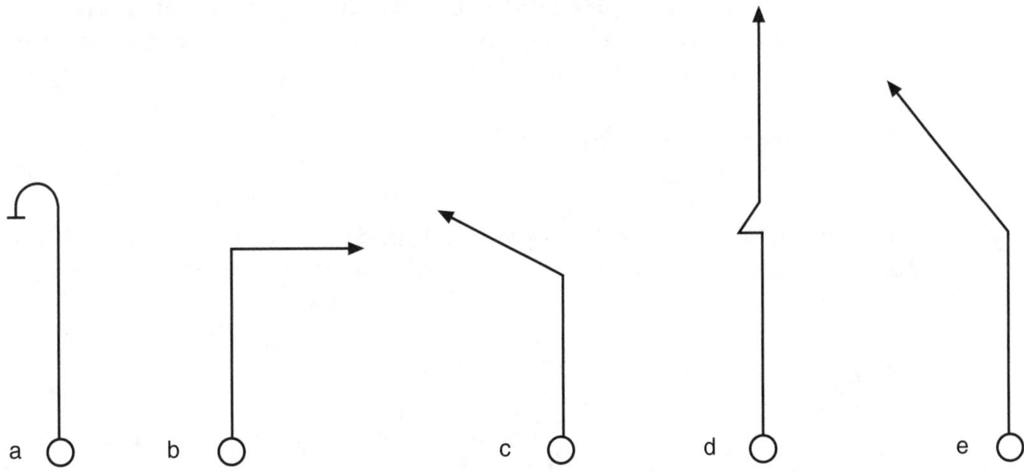

Figure 8.2 Pass patterns: *(a)* curl, *(b)* square-out, *(c)* slant, *(d)* streak, *(e)* post.

Run-and-Shoot Offense

Flag football affords a great opportunity to use a run-and-shoot offense, because there is a lot of room for passing the ball with relatively few players on the field. In this offense, the receivers respond to the defensive coverage and "shoot" to the open area. (This offense is geared more to 6- and 7-year-olds than to younger kids.) It's an exciting offense that calls for a quarterback with a strong arm and the ability to find the open receiver and for receivers who can read the defense and find the open seams on the field.

Defensive Tactics

Your defensive approach should reflect the talents of your players. Your basic defensive alignment must capitalize on their strengths and compensate for their weaknesses. For example, if you have a somewhat big, slow team, you will want your defensive backs to not play too tight on the offensive receivers.

The three most important goals a defense can strive to accomplish are

- to prevent the easy touchdown,
- to get possession of the ball, and
- to score.

In addition, you'll want to teach players how to play player-to-player and zone defenses. We'll look at the three goals first and then explore the different types of defenses.

Prevent the Easy Touchdown

Although the obvious objective of defensive flag football is to keep the opposition from scoring, a more functional objective of defensive play is to prevent the opposition from scoring the easy touchdown with a long pass (or long run after a short pass). Make your opponent earn every point it scores by having a defense that challenges every yard. Praise players for preventing first downs and stopping the opponent's drives downfield.

Get Possession of the Ball

The defensive team may gain possession of the ball by preventing the opponent from gaining the next first down on four downs, forcing a "punt" (punt situations are handled at the YMCA Rookies level by a method other than kicking the ball, as explained in chapter 9), or intercepting a pass.

Score

The defense can score by returning an intercepted pass. Remember that all fumbles are dead at the spot to avoid pileups and subsequent injuries. The defense also can score by pulling the flag of the ball carrier in his or her end zone for a safety.

Player-to-Player Defense

In a player-to-player defense, each player on the defense is assigned a specific offensive player to cover. This defense works best when you have athletic players with speed and the ability to not get beat. Inexperienced or slower players tend to get beat more often in one-on-one situations, leading to big gains or scores for the other team.

Think in terms of who you are playing, too: if the receivers are fast and athletic, you may want to play a zone defense to lessen the risk of getting beat for a big play.

Zone Defense

In a zone defense, each defensive player is assigned to cover a certain area of the field. A zone can help guard against big plays; defensive help is never too far away. Mistakes made in zone defenses often are not as costly as those made in player-to-player defenses. A disadvantage of using a zone is that the opponent can overload a zone; in this case the defender in that zone should cover the deepest offensive player in the zone until the ball is thrown to a different player.

Offensive Skills

The offensive skills you will want to teach your players are stance, throwing (playing quarterback), and receiving.

Stance

The stance is the proper alignment of a player's body to start each play. Before the snap, offensive players should stand with their weight on the balls of their feet with their knees bent and their backs straight. All offensive players should use a two-point stance, as follows:

- Place the feet shoulder-width apart, in a heel-toe relationship, with the foot closest to the football back slightly more than the other.
- Keep the back straight, leaning forward slightly.
- Square the shoulders to the line of scrimmage.
- Hold the arms in a comfortable position.

Figure 8.3 illustrates how this stance should look.

Figure 8.3 Proper stance.

Playing Quarterback

You'll need to teach your quarterbacks how to play out of the shotgun formation and how to throw passes.

Shotgun Formation

Quarterbacks start in the shotgun formation. They line up about 5 yards behind the center. They should look at the defense and scan the field for particular defensive formations. That will enable them to see who might be open.

Throwing the Football

Quarterbacks should keep the ball in the ready position at the armpit before raising it straight up to throw. They should grip the ball with the fingers over the laces and the index finger close to the tip of the football to guide it, leaving some space between the palm and the football (see figure 8.4a). They should extend the elbow out and lead the ball toward the throw (see figure 8.4b). They should release the ball with the thumb and the wrist facing down. On release, the index finger should be last to leave the football, and it should be pointed directly toward the target (see figure 8.4c).

a b c

Figure 8.4 Proper throwing form for quarterback.

Receiving

Receiving involves running patterns and catching the football.

Running Patterns

When the quarterback calls a play in the huddle, the receiver knows what pattern to run. The quarterback selects this pattern from many options on a pass tree (see figure 8.1 on page 117).

The most important thing you should teach receivers is to explode off the line of scrimmage. They should run to the outside shoulder of the defensive back, forcing defenders to turn their shoulders parallel to the line of scrimmage to cover them. Next, receivers must come under control at the breaking point of the pattern. They then plant a foot, turn the head and shoulders, and react to the football.

Catching the Football

The next step in coaching receivers is to teach them how to catch the football. This is a matter of concentration and dedication. Receivers should watch the football into their hands. If the football is thrown high, receivers should catch it with thumbs together (see figure 8.5); if it is thrown low, receivers should catch it with little fingers together (see figure 8.6). Also, teach receivers to catch the football in their hands and not trap it against their bodies.

Give receivers ample opportunities to catch every type of pass that they will see. Instruct receivers to tuck the ball under the arm and protect it after making the catch. Success will help the receivers gain confidence, and first downs and touchdowns reinforce that catching the ball is fun.

Figure 8.5 Catching a high pass.

Figure 8.6 Catching a low pass.

Defensive Skills

Playing defense is part instinct, part effort, and part technique. You can't do much about your players' instincts, and most young players love the game, so effort isn't a problem. What a flag football coach *can* do is teach and develop players' defensive skills. The rest of this chapter will focus on defensive stance, pulling the flag, rushing the passer, and covering receivers.

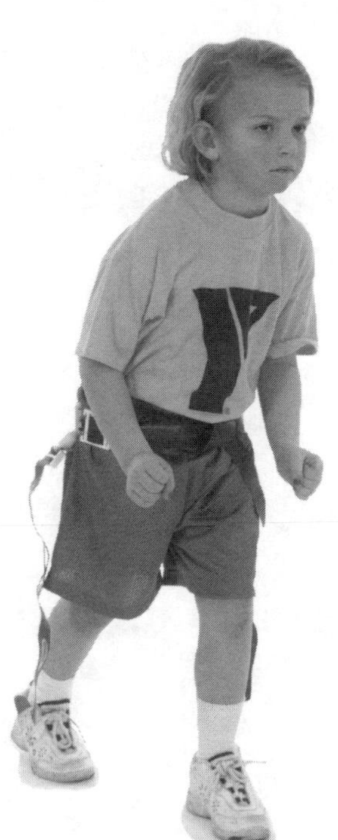

Figure 8.7 Proper stance for linebacker.

Stance

The proper initial alignment of the body for the defensive player is very important. Teach the defensive line players, linebackers, and defensive backs the proper stances for their respective positions.

Defensive Line Players

The stance for defensive line players is the same as that for the offensive line players. Before the play, defensive line players should stand with their weight on the balls of their feet, knees bent, and backs straight, ready to move on the play.

Linebackers

The linebacker should have a good balanced stance, with feet shoulder-width apart and slightly staggered. Figure 8.7 shows the proper stance for a linebacker. Teach your linebackers the following points:

- Bend your knees slightly to ensure low body position.
- Focus your eyes on the player you are to defend.
- Have one foot slightly forward; step with this foot first as you react to the key and find the football.

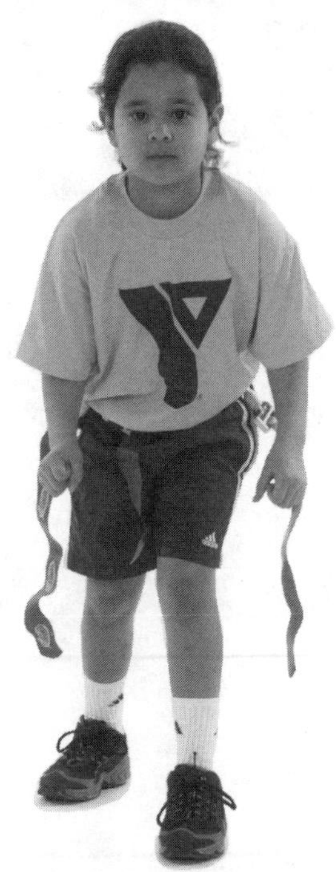

Figure 8.8 Proper stance for defensive back.

Defensive Backs

Coach the defensive backs to line up with a slightly staggered stance in a relaxed position. Figure 8.8 shows the proper stance for a defensive back. Instruct your players as follows:

- Keep your feet slightly staggered, with the outside foot back.
- Point the toes straight ahead.
- Focus eyes on the player you are to key.
- Assume a slightly crouching position, with your knees slightly bent.
- Take a short step on the snap and then react to the play.

Pulling the Flag

If you want to have a good defensive team in flag football, you must teach your defensive players to pull flags. Players who learn the correct fundamentals of flag pulling early can more easily develop skills as they get older.

Figure 8.9 Proper flag-pulling technique.

Head-On Flag Pull

The head-on flag pull is used when defensive players are lined up straight across from the offensive player coming toward them. Keep low and center your attention on the ball carrier's waist. Figure 8.9 illustrates proper flag-pulling technique. Emphasize the following points to your flag pullers:

- Make sure that you are under control so as not to overrun the ball carrier or dive and miss the flag pull.
- Maintain a wide, balanced stance; keep the feet moving with choppy steps.
- Extend your arms and head in front of your body.
- Keep your head up, your back arched, and your knees slightly bent.
- Slide your body to one side to avoid contact and reach for the flag.
- Always wrap around your opponent, but do not hold. As you wrap around, attempt to pull both flags.

Angle Flag Pull

This flag pull is necessary when the ball carrier runs a wide play or gets close to the sideline. Coach your defensive players using these guidelines:

- Keep under control and be ready to move in any direction.
- Maintain a good balanced stance and stay on your feet with your head up.
- Reach for the flag with your body under control, head up, eyes focused on the ball carrier's waist or numbers.
- Stay relaxed as you pull the flag.

Open-Field Flag Pull

After the runner has cleared the line of scrimmage or when a receiver has caught the football and has just one player to beat, the defender must use the open-field flag pull. Coach your players that in the open field the most important thing to do is get close enough to the ball carrier that they can pull the flag. Stress these coaching points:

- Keep under control with your legs bent.
- Keep your feet moving, head up, and arms out away from your body.
- Use the sideline to your advantage, penning in or getting an angle on the runner.
- Your sole responsibility is to prevent the score by pulling the flag.

Covering Receivers

The defense must be able to cover the receivers to stop the offense from moving the ball through the air. Spend time training your players to defend the pass. Following are some of the necessary skills.

Proper Alignment

The defensive corners (cornerbacks) should line up 5 to 7 yards off the wide receivers. The safeties should line up 8 to 12 yards deep off the line of scrimmage. If you are playing only one safety, he or she should line up deep in the middle of the field.

Drop Step

Instruct your players to bend at the waist with a forward body lean. The drop step should start with a step backward with the back foot and a push off the front foot. As players turn, they are running sideways at a 45-degree angle. Their arms should move in a normal, relaxed running fashion. Players should be under control so that when receivers make their break to catch the ball, defenders are ready to drive on them.

Player-to-Player Coverage

Looking at figure 8.10, use the following guidelines to teach your players how to cover receivers:

- Keep your eyes focused primarily on the receiver you are covering (at the belt region).
- Maintain a 3- to 4-yard cushion between you and the receiver.
- Never turn your back on the receiver.
- Once the ball is in the air, play it aggressively.

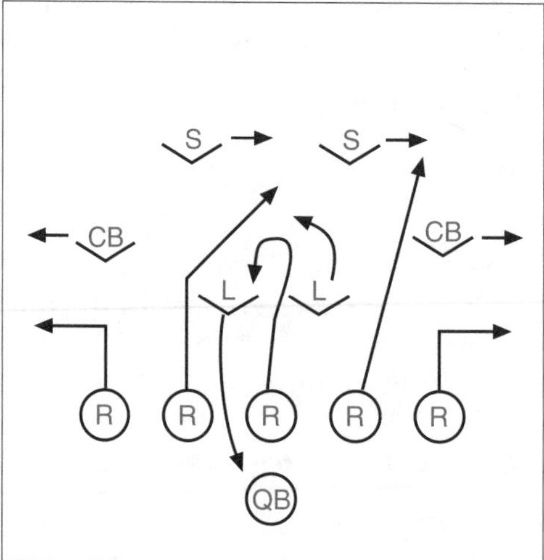

Figure 8.10 Player-to-player coverage.

Zone Coverage

Teams use zone coverage extensively because of the speed of the game and because flag football is predominantly a passing game. A relatively inexperienced player can more easily learn the game and its techniques by playing zone rather than player-to-player. Figure 8.11 shows an example of zone coverage. Use the following guidelines to teach your players how to play a zone and cover receivers:

- Keep your eyes open and your head up to be alert for players running into your zone.
- Maintain a 3- or 4-yard cushion between you and the receiver.
- Never turn your back on the receiver.
- Once the ball is in the air, play it aggressively.

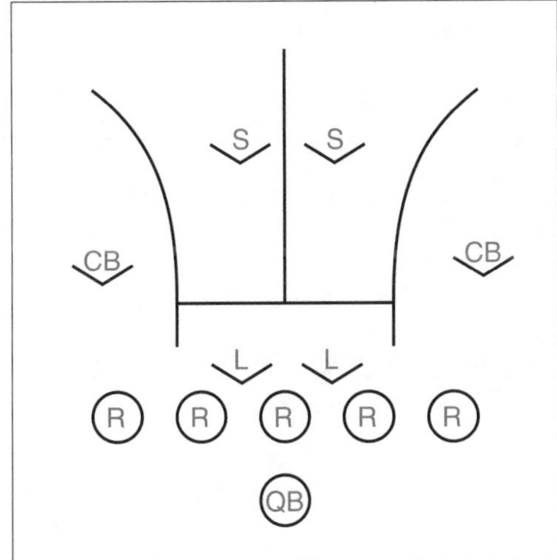

Figure 8.11 Zone coverage.

chapter

9

Teaching Flag Football Rules and Traditions

Here we'll introduce you to some of the basic rules and traditions of flag football. Even though you won't be playing against other teams in YMCA Rookies, it's important to know and pass on the rules—and play by them during practice—so that your players will be ready for competition when they enter YMCA Winners. We won't try to cover all the rules of the game, but we'll give you what you need to work with 4- to 7-year-old children. Some of the rules will be explained just so that you understand the game better. Those you should teach your players have already been incorporated into the practice plans.

In this chapter, we'll give you information on appropriate ball size and field size and markings, player equipment, how to play the game, positions, rules, violations and penalties, and scoring. (We don't cover time elements, such as game length or timeouts, because at this level you won't be playing in games against other teams.) In a short section, we'll show you the officiating signals for flag football. We also will talk briefly about a few of the unwritten rules or traditions of flag football, which good players follow to be courteous and safe.

Before we discuss rules, though, let's start by defining some flag football terms.

Terms to Know

Flag football has its own vocabulary. Being familiar with common terms will make your job easier.

- End zone—That area bounded by the goal line, end line, and sidelines (see figure 9.1).
- First down—The first of four allotted downs the offensive team receives. The offense must gain 10 yards within those four plays to maintain possession of the ball.
- Fumble—Flag football has no fumbles. Once the ball hits the ground during a play, it is ruled dead at the spot, with the team last in possession retaining possession.
- Interception—Gaining possession of the ball; it occurs when a defender catches a pass thrown by the offense.
- Line of scrimmage—The line from which a play starts. The line of scrimmage stretches from one sideline to the other, passing through the point of the ball nearest the defense.
- Possession—Having control of the ball.
- Pulling the flag—The legal removal of a flag from an opponent in possession of the ball.

Rule Modifications

In table 9.1 we present rules that cover some basics of the game.

TABLE 9.1

Rule Modifications for Flag Football

Players on field per team	6
Players on team	12
Ball size	10 1/4 to 10 1/2 inches long (or nerf ball)
Field size	30 × 60 yards plus two end zones 30 × 10 yards each (see figure 9.1)
Yards needed for 1st down	10 yards

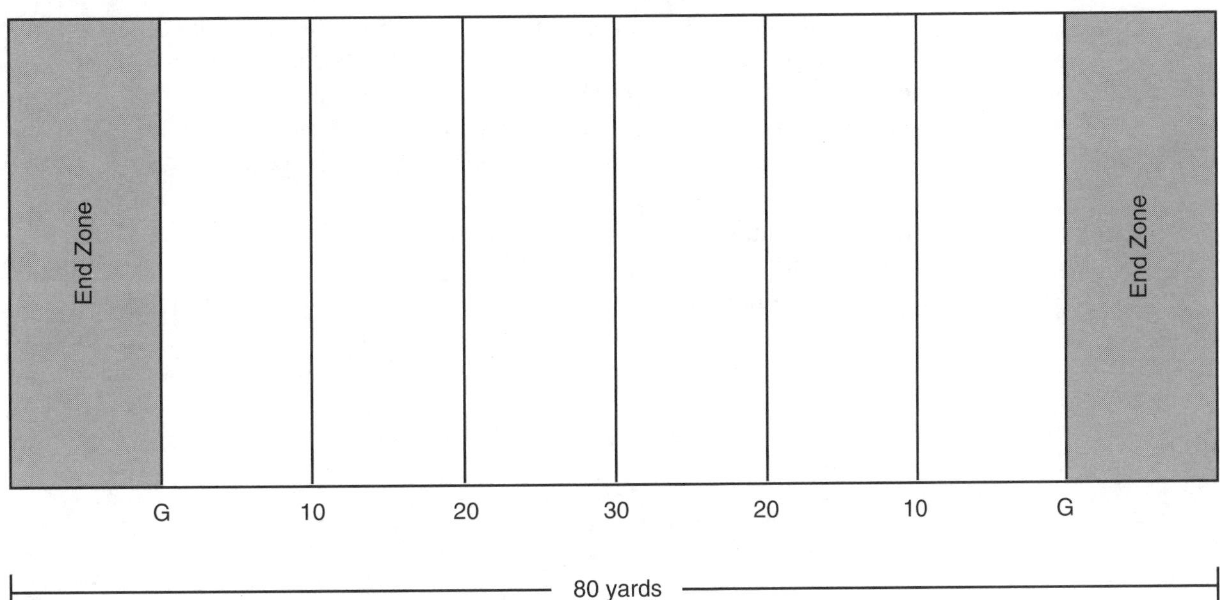

Figure 9.1 Flag football field.

 Player Equipment

Flag football requires very little equipment. Players should wear a T-shirt or jersey, keeping it tucked in so that other players don't injure their hands when they reach for the flag. They also should wear shorts or football pants with only knee pads, as well as socks and shoes. The shoes can be either tennis shoes or shoes with plastic (not metal) cleats. Each player must have a flag belt and should receive two flags for play, which are worn one on each side.

One piece of safety equipment that players should have is a mouthguard, to prevent injury to the teeth or mouth. Players should not wear watches, rings, necklaces, or other jewelry that could injure them or other players.

 How the Game Is Played

The five offensive teammates of the quarterback line up on the line of scrimmage and wait for the quarterback to start the play. The defense is lined up facing them. The quarterback holds the ball and says, "Ready," which allows one of the players to go into motion; he or she then says, "Go!" and the play begins. All offensive players run pass patterns; all are eligible to receive passes. At the YMCA Rookies level, there is no blocking. One defensive player only can rush the quarterback; this player cannot rush for 5 seconds after the quarterback says "Go!" To mark the 5 seconds, the coach counts the seconds aloud ("one-thousand one, one-thousand two, one-thousand three . . .").

The quarterback *cannot* run with the ball; he or she *must* pass the ball. On a completed pass, the receiver tries to advance the ball as far as possible toward the other team's goal line. The defense tries to pull the ball carrier's flag to keep the offense from advancing down the field. When this happens, the coach whistles the ball dead and momentarily stops play.

Play resumes at the new line of scrimmage (where the ball was downed). The offense is allowed four plays, or downs, to make a first down. They make a first down by advancing the ball at least 10 yards from the original line of scrimmage (where it was on first down). If the offense makes a first down, they are given a new set of four plays. They maintain possession of the ball until one of four things happens:

- They do not advance the ball at least 10 yards within their allotted four downs
- They elect to turn the ball over to the defense by "punting" (see "Kicking and Punting" on page 131.)
- The defense intercepts a pass
- The offense scores a touchdown

Player Positions

At the YMCA Rookies level, only a few positions are needed. On offense, there is a quarterback and five receivers. At the quarterback position you'll want a good communicator and a good athlete who can handle many responsibilities. He or she also should have an excellent throwing arm. We recommend that you allow all players to play quarterback in practice, however.

The basic positions on defense are defensive line players, linebackers, and defensive backs.

- **Defensive line players**—The defensive line players are strong and quick players whose responsibilities include rushing the quarterback (only one defender can rush on any one play) and playing receivers near the line of scrimmage.
- **Linebackers**—Linebackers must be strong and quick, with a keen sense of timing, because they are in the middle of almost every play on defense.
- **Defensive backs**—The defensive backs must be quick, agile, and strong enough to be able to cover and react to the ball. Cornerbacks and safeties are defensive backs.

Rules of Play

A number of flag football rules have been added or modified to make the game more appropriate for the YMCA Rookies age groups. Use these rules for all practice games.

Starting a Play

Each team must have six players on the field. Before the play, receivers on the line must be within 5 yards of the ball laterally, and all offensive players must be set for at least 1 second prior to when the quarterback says, "Ready." No player should use a three- or four-point stance; such stances put players in a dangerous position, as they aren't wearing helmets.

Passing

Every play must be a pass play; there are no running plays. All passes must be forward and must be received beyond the line of scrimmage. Shovel passes (underhand passes) are allowed but must be received beyond the line of scrimmage. Interceptions may be returned.

Running

There are no direct running plays. Players can only run downfield with the ball after receiving a pass. Blocks are not allowed. No laterals or pitches of any kind are allowed. Spinning is allowed, but players cannot dive to avoid a defensive player. Offensive players are not permitted to guard their flags by making contact with defensive players who are trying to remove their flags. Stiff-arms are illegal.

Receiving

All offensive players are eligible to receive forward passes (including the quarterback if the ball has been handed off behind the line of scrimmage). All passes must be thrown from behind the line of scrimmage. Only one player is allowed to be in motion when the quarterback says, "Ready." Any contact made by receivers on the line must be made with arms in and hands closed. A player must have at least one foot inbounds when making a reception.

Kicking and Punting

Field goals, extra points (kicking for points after a touchdown), and kickoffs are not allowed. Also, players do not actually punt. But the offense can elect to "punt" on fourth down by informing the coach; the coach then will move the ball 15 yards downfield, where the opponents will take over on first down. If the offense is within 15 yards of the defenders' goal line, the coach will move the ball half the distance to the goal line.

Dead Balls

The ball is "dead" if a defensive player removes one flag from the offensive player's waist and immediately holds the flag up above his or her head so that the coach can see where the flag pull occurred. The ball is placed where the ball carrier's feet were when the flag was pulled, not where the ball was. A ball also is "dead" when the ball carrier steps out of bounds, the ball carrier's knee hits the ground, or a touchdown or a safety is scored. The defense cannot pick up a fumble; the ball is down where it hits the ground and remains with the offense. Substitutions may be made on any dead ball.

Defense

Any player who rushes the passer must wait for the coach's audible 5-second count after the quarterback says, "Go" to rush. Only one player can rush the quarterback. Defensive players may use their hands to push through the line, but they cannot hold or grasp the ball carrier in attempting to remove the flag.

Pushing, striking, holding, slapping, or tripping a player when attempting to pull a flag is not permitted. Defensive players may leave their feet to pull a flag. If an offensive player's flag inadvertently falls to the ground, a two-handed tag between the shoulders and knees by a defensive player constitutes a flag pull.

When the flag is clearly taken from the player with the ball, the down is over, and the ball is declared dead. The player who removes the flag should immediately hold the flag above his or her head to help the coach find the spot where the removal occurred. A defensive player may not remove a flag from an offensive player who does not have possession of the ball.

Violations and Penalties

The following are game violations, which will result in a penalty to the team that commits the violation.

Defense

- Offsides—5 yards, enforced from the line of scrimmage
- Defensive pass interference—10 yards and a first down, enforced from the point of the foul
- Defensive holding or illegal use of hands—5 yards and an automatic first down, enforced from the point of the foul
- Illegal removal of the flag—10 yards and an automatic first down, enforced from the point of the foul
- Illegal rushing—10 yards and an automatic first down

If the offensive team has a breakaway and a defensive player tackles to get him or her out of bounds, the coach may award a touchdown.

Offense

- Offsides—5 yards, enforced from the line of scrimmage
- Illegal procedure or formation—5 yards, enforced from the line of scrimmage
- Blocking—5 yards and down over (at the YMCA Rookies level, blocking is illegal)

- Backfield in motion—5 yards, enforced from the line of scrimmage
- Illegal forward pass—10 yards, enforced from the line of scrimmage
- Offensive holding—10 yards, enforced from the line of scrimmage
- Offensive pass inference—10 yards and a loss of a down, enforced from the line of scrimmage
- Flag guarding—10 yards and a loss of a down, enforced from the point of the foul
- Intentionally grounded pass—5 yards and a loss of a down, enforced from the point of the foul
- Stiff-arming—10 yards and the loss of a down, enforced from the point of the foul
- Illegal use of hands—10 yards, enforced from the line of scrimmage
- Clipping—10 yards, enforced from the line of scrimmage

General

- Loose clothing—5 yards, enforced from the line of scrimmage
- Unnecessary roughness—10 yards, plus a loss of a down if by the offense or an automatic first down if by the defense, enforced from the point of the foul
- Unsporting conduct—10 yards, enforced from the line of scrimmage

For flagrant fouls, the player is first given a warning. If the player commits a second flagrant foul, he or she is ejected from that game and the next game. The same holds for "trash talking"—any talk that may be offensive to others. Only the team captain may ask the referee questions about rule clarification and interpretations. Players cannot question judgment calls. Games cannot end on a defensive penalty, unless the offense declines it.

Scoring

Points can be scored in the following ways:

- Touchdown—A player in control of the ball touches or crosses the vertical plane of the opponent's goal line. It is worth six points.
- Point after touchdown —A player receives a pass in the end zone or runs with the passed ball into the end zone from the 10-yard or 3-yard line. If the ball is placed on the 3-yard line, the play is worth one point; if the ball is placed on the 10-yard line, the play is worth two points.
- Safety—An offensive player loses the ball out of bounds in his or her own end zone or has his or her flag pulled in his or her own end zone. It counts for two points for the defense.

Officiating Signals

Even though your YMCA Rookies flag football practices won't be officiated, you may want to use the officiating signals to indicate fouls or violations. If you use the correct signals, the players will get used to the signals and their meanings. Figure 9.2 shows some common officiating signals.

a b c

d e f

Figure 9.2 Officiating signals for *(a)* timeout, *(b)* touchdown, *(c)* personal foul, *(d)* illegal use of hands, *(e)* illegal contact, *(f)* delay of game, *(g)* offsides, *(h)* holding, *(i)* illegal motion, *(j)* first down, *(k)* pass interference, *(l)* incomplete pass, penalty refused, or point(s) after touchdown attempt no good, *(m)* flag guarding.

g
h
i
j
k
l
m

Flag Football Traditions

Young children need to know only a couple of unwritten rules for flag football, and both of these are based on the core values. First, players should be honest if they know they committed a violation but aren't called for it. This is especially important in YMCA Rookies games because an official won't be watching. Being truthful about calls is an example of being honest.

Second, players should play cooperatively with their teammates and their opponents. This exemplifies showing respect for others.

chapter

10

Teaching Fitness and Safety

As a coach you have a great opportunity to teach your players not only about flag football but also about fitness and health. The attitudes and the knowledge they learn now can be a foundation for their future fitness. And you don't have to be a fitness expert to do this. We've supplied you with ideas for discussion in the Fitness Circles in the practice plans. To give you more background information, we'll discuss some basics of health and fitness in this chapter. We'll begin with the components of fitness and continue with some general training principles and how they relate to fitness. We'll end this section by listing some healthy habits children should develop.

You are also responsible for the safety of your players while they are under your care, so we mention some specific precautions you can take. As accidents may happen no matter how careful you are, though, we also list the steps you should take to be prepared to provide basic emergency care for injuries to players and describe some first-aid procedures for minor injuries and heat illnesses.

We conclude the chapter with a brief summary of the legal duties you must fulfill as a coach.

Components of Fitness

The main components of fitness you need to know about as a YMCA Rookies coach are these:

- Cardiorespiratory fitness
- Muscular strength and endurance
- Flexibility

Cardiorespiratory Fitness

As you might guess from the term, *cardiorespiratory fitness* is fitness of the heart (cardio) and circulatory system and the lungs (respiratory). It's also known as *aerobic fitness.* Training for cardiorespiratory fitness involves moving large muscle groups (the legs and arms) in a rhythmic activity that is sustained for at least several minutes and uses large amounts of oxygen. Activities such as running, swimming, or bicycling are good examples of cardiorespiratory training activities. Such training improves the transportation of oxygen through the blood to working muscles by making the heart and lungs more efficient and the body better able to use the oxygen when it reaches the muscles. Someone who has cardiorespiratory fitness can engage in endurance activities without feeling winded or getting tired easily.

Some of the concepts related to cardiorespiratory fitness that you can communicate to young children are these:

- Physical activity (such as flag football) is good for fitness.
- The heart is a muscle that pumps our blood. It can be strengthened by exercise.
- Our hearts beat faster when we exercise.

Encourage your players to be active at home, whether with flag football or other forms of physical activity.

Muscular Strength and Endurance

Muscles can be fit in two ways: they can be strong, and they can have endurance:

- *Strength* is the ability of a muscle to exert force against resistance, such as a weight. We use strength to perform everyday tasks such as lifting a grocery bag or opening a door.
- *Endurance* is the ability of a muscle to exercise for an extended period of time without too much fatigue. It's useful in performing tasks that require repeated movements, such as vacuuming a carpet or washing a car.

Muscular strength and endurance can be improved with strength training, but (unless you have players who are so unusually weak that they have difficulty playing) strength training is not necessary for 4- to 7-year-old children. It is more appropriate for older youths who want to train more seriously for the sport.

Some of the concepts related to muscular strength and endurance that your players will be able to understand are these:

- We use many of our muscles when we play flag football.
- Using muscles during flag football may increase muscular endurance.
- When we move in different directions, we use different sets of muscles.

Flexibility

Flexibility involves the joints and muscles. It is the ability of the muscles around a joint to allow the joint its full range of motion. Being flexible makes movement easier.

For adults, stretching helps make muscles more flexible. While it's not really known if stretching is effective for children, we do advocate devoting a small amount of time to stretching before and after play. In this way, children also learn the proper techniques for stretching, which are as follows:

- Warm up with 5 to 10 minutes of low-intensity aerobic activity.
- Perform two repetitions of each stretch.
- Stretch to the point of a gentle pull, then hold the stretch for 10 counts without bouncing.
- For cooling down, walk around to allow the heart and breathing rates to return to normal. Then perform three to five repetitions of each stretch before the muscles cool.

The following list provides two exercises that can be used to improve flexibility.

1. **Quadriceps Stretch**—Place a hand on the wall (or partner's shoulder). Bend one leg and hold it by the ankle. Move the thigh backwards slightly. Repeat with the other leg. This exercise stretches the muscles on the front of the thigh.

2. **Modified Hamstring Stretch**—Sit on the floor with your left leg straight and your right leg bent. Tuck your right foot against your upper left thigh. Bend from the waist, reach forward, and clasp your lower leg (left ankle if possible). Bring your chest toward your left knee. Hold. Repeat with the right leg. This exercise stretches the muscle on the back of your extended leg (thigh) and the muscle on the front of your bent leg (thigh).

Training Principles

You need to know just a few principles of training to work with players at this age level:

- The warm-up/cool-down principle
- The overload principle
- The reversibility principle
- The specificity principle

Warm-Up/Cool-Down Principle

Before beginning strenuous activity, players should perform some moderate warm-up activity that will increase body temperature, respiration, and heart rate and help prevent muscle and tendon strains and ligament sprains. Warm-up activities might be calisthenics, stretching, or any games with small numbers of players or skill drills that are not strenuous. Try to use warm-up activities that are interesting to your players.

A sample warm-up routine you can use with your players follows.

- Have all children stand in a circle.
- Spend 20 to 30 seconds on each exercise.
- Have the children start walking in a circle to their right. As they walk, have them do the following exercises:
    1. Walk—high arm swings
    2. Walk—roll shoulders
    3. Walk—cross-body arm swings
    4. Walk—high knee action
    5. Change directions—high knee action
    6. Jog
    7. Side shuffle
    8. Side step right
    9. Side step left
- Have the children jog for a few minutes.

The following list provides a few other warm-up exercises that could be used to get ready to play flag football.

1. Giant Arm Circles: While walking, have your arms describe giant circles backwards. Do these arm movements slowly and deliberately.
2. Heel-Toe Raise: Stand with feet close together and your hands on your hips. Raise up on your toes and then your heels. This exercise stretches (warms up) the lower leg muscles.
3. Low Back Stretch: Lie on your back with your knees pulled up toward your chest. This exercise helps stretch the low back muscles.

Once strenuous activity is over, players should then slow down gradually with a cool-down activity. Stopping heavy activity abruptly can cause blood to pool in the legs and feet and can slow the removal of waste products created by muscle use. Light activity such as walking or stretching helps to keep blood circulating.

A sample cool-down routine you can use with your players follows.

- Spend 20 to 30 seconds on each exercise
- Have the children walk in a circle to their right

1. Walk—alternate high arm swings
2. Walk—cross-body arm swings
3. Walk—shake arms and fingers vigorously
4. Walk—shake legs
5. Walk—giant arm circles
6. Change direction
7. Walk on toes
8. Walk on heels
9. Walk—shake arms and legs

- Have the children stretch for a few minutes.

1. **Side stretch**—Stand with feet shoulder-width apart, and legs straight. Place one hand on your hip and extend your other hand up over your head. Bend to the side that has your hand on your hip. Move slowly. Hold for 15 seconds and repeat on the other side.
2. **Modified Hamstring Stretch**—Sit on the floor with your left leg straight and your right leg bent. Tuck your right foot against your upper left thigh. Bend from the waist, reach forward, and clasp your lower leg (left ankle if possible). Bring your chest toward your left knee. Hold. Repeat with the right leg.
3. **Quadriceps Stretch**—Place a hand on the wall (or partner's shoulder). Bend one leg and hold it by the ankle. Move the thigh backwards slightly. Repeat with the other leg.
4. **Kneeling Shoulder Stretch**—Kneel on the floor. Sit back on your heels and look at your knees as you reach forward with your hands. Keep your seat down and continue to focus on your knees. When you have reached as far as possible, press down against the floor with your hands. You will feel your shoulders stretch. Hold and repeat.

Overload Principle

Luckily for us, our bodies are adaptable. We can present them with a workload a bit higher than what we've done before, and they will, over time, adapt to it. Each time our bodies adapt, we can then add more to what we've done before. This is how we can improve our fitness.

Overloading the body can be done in three different ways:

- Frequency—doing an activity more often
- Intensity—doing an activity harder
- Time—doing an activity longer

To remember these methods of overloading, think of the acronym FIT. Increasing one or more of these aspects of activity or exercise will put a heavier load on the body.

This principle can be used in all kinds of training. A weightlifter could add more weight as she grows stronger, adding intensity. A runner might add more miles or hours of training, adding time. Either one might choose to exercise more often during the week, increasing the frequency.

Overloading stimulates the body to make changes. Such changes involve the nervous system, which becomes able to recruit more muscle fibers; the circulation, which becomes better at distributing the blood to the working muscles; and the muscles, which produce new protein to meet working demands.

Here is a list of a few exercises that will help your muscles get stronger.

1. **Push-ups**—Lie face down on the floor with your feet together and your hands beneath your shoulders. Keeping your body straight, extend your arms fully, then return to the starting position. See how many you can do, up to 10. This exercise helps develop the shoulders, chest, and arms. (If children have difficulty, let them do the push-ups from their knees.)

2. **Partner Pull-ups**—One partner stands with legs spread apart. The second partner lies flat on his back, arms fully extended, grasping the forearms of the standing partner. With heels resting on the floor and the body rigid, the second partner should pull his/her upper body toward the partner by flexing his/her arms until his/her chest comes to the height of the partner's knees. This exercise strengthens the arm, shoulder, and chest muscles. Do as many as you can do, up to 10.

3. **Abdominal Curls**—Lie on your back with your knees bent and feet on the floor, shoulder-width apart. Place your arms across your chest and hands on opposite shoulders. Curl your head and shoulders upward off the floor until the elbows touch the thighs, keeping the arms in contact with the chest. Then lower your upper body until your shoulder blades touch the floor. Do as many as you can, up to 10. (Some children may have difficulty with this exercise, not so much because of weak abdominal muscles, but because their heads are much larger in proportion to their bodies [compared with adults] and therefore, they are at a physical disadvantage.)

Here's one caution about overloads—don't increase them too quickly, or you could cause injuries. A gradual approach is always safer.

Reversibility Principle

To state this principle briefly, use it or lose it! Just as the body can make adaptations when given an overload, it can also lose its capabilities when it is not used. It takes three times as long to gain endurance as it does to lose it. If you stayed in bed for a week, you would lose nearly 10 percent of your aerobic fitness. Your strength would also decline, although not as fast. This is why you want to encourage your players to be active both during and after the season.

Specificity Principle

This principle simply means that the type of training a person chooses to do should relate to his or her goal. For example, heavy weight training will not make a runner run faster. Bicycling will not improve swimming performance as much as additional swimming would. Performance improves most when the training done is specific to the desired activity.

Healthy Habits

One of the better things you can do for your players is to instill healthy habits. Being healthy is a lot easier when it becomes a routine part of life. Talk to your players about the benefits of being fit and eating well.

General Fitness

With all the distractions of video games and TV, many children are less active than they might otherwise be. Make a point of explaining to your players that being active will help them be healthier and feel better. It also may help their game!

Also discuss how other good health habits can help them, such as getting enough sleep, brushing their teeth and washing well, and saying no to tobacco, alcohol, and other drugs.

Good Nutrition

Good nutrition is not the first thing most young children think about when they choose foods. Young children may not even know which foods are good for them and which are not. You can start to make them aware of which foods will make them healthier and why good nutrition is important.

A simple guide for a good diet is the U.S. Department of Agriculture's food pyramid (see figure 10.1). This is a guide that encourages us to eat lots of breads, cereals, rice, pasta, vegetables, and fruits; a smaller amount of meat, cheese, eggs, dried beans, or nuts; and only a very little bit of fats, oils, and sweets. Eating this way cuts down on the amount of fats in the diet and helps ensure an adequate amount of vitamins and minerals.

A serving of the foods in these groups is equal to the following amounts:

- 1/2 cup of a fruit or vegetable
- 3/4 cup of juice
- 1 slice of bread
- 1 cup of milk
- 1 average-sized piece of fruit
- 1 cup of salad greens
- 1/2 cup of cooked pasta
- Lean meat about the size of a deck of cards

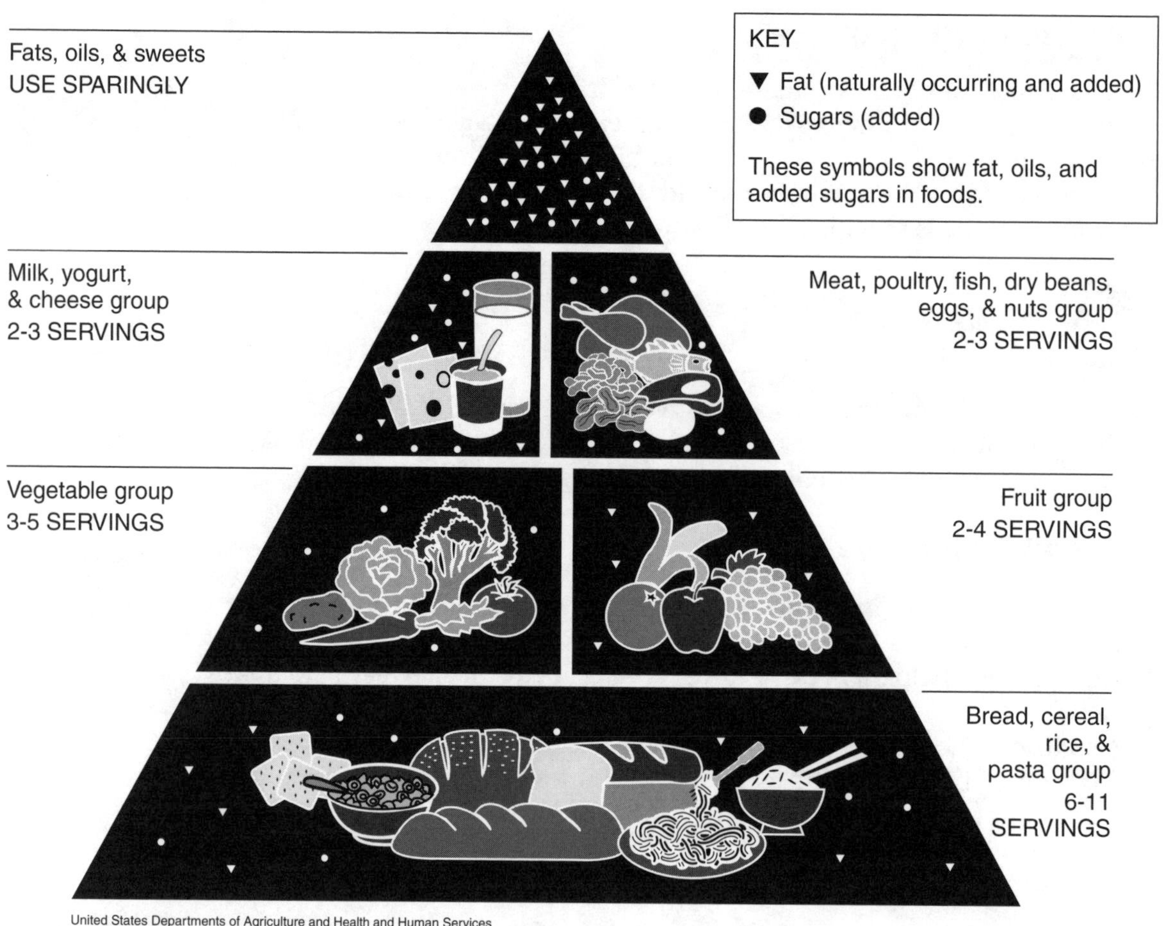

Figure 10.1 The food guide pyramid.

According to Kalish (1996), the number of servings children should eat depends on their age, height, weight, and level of physical activity. One exception is milk; children need three milk-group servings a day.

Safety Precautions

As a coach you're morally and legally responsible for the safety of your players during practice sessions and games. You need to take some regular precautions to ensure their safety. Some simple ways that you can protect your players from harm are having players get a preseason physical exam, inspecting equipment and facilities regularly, matching athletes by maturity, warning players and their parents of the potential for injury, supervising properly and keeping good records, and adjusting practices and games according to environmental conditions.

Preseason Physical Examination

We recommend that your players have a physical examination before participating in YMCA Rookies flag football. The exam should address the most likely areas of medical concern and identify youngsters at high risk. See appendix B, "Preparticipation Screening for YMCA Youth Super Sports Programs," for specific information on what should take place during the preseason physical examination. We also suggest that you have players' parents or guardians sign a participation agreement form and a release form to allow their children to be treated in case of an emergency.

Regular Inspection of Equipment and Facilities

Check the quality and fit of all of the equipment used by your players at the beginning of the season and inspect the equipment regularly during the season. Worn-out, damaged, lost, or outdated equipment must be replaced immediately.

Remember, also, to examine regularly the field on which your players practice and play. Remove hazards, report conditions you cannot remedy, and request maintenance as necessary. If unsafe conditions exist, either make adaptations to avoid risk to your players' safety or stop the practice or game until safe conditions have been restored.

Matching Athletes by Maturity

Children of the same age may differ in height and weight by up to 6 inches and 50 pounds. That's why in contact sports or sports in which size provides an advantage, it's essential to match players against opponents of similar size and physical maturity. Such an approach gives smaller, less mature children a better chance to succeed and avoid injury, and it provides larger children with more of a challenge.

Informing Players and Parents of Inherent Risks

You are legally responsible for warning players of the inherent risks involved in playing flag football. "Failure to warn" is one of the most successful arguments in lawsuits against coaches. Therefore, thoroughly explain the inherent risks of flag football, and make sure each player knows, understands, and appreciates those risks.

The preseason parent-orientation meeting is a good opportunity to explain the risks of the sport to parents and players. It is also a good occasion on which to have both the players and their parents sign waivers releasing you from liability should an injury occur. Such waivers do not relieve you of responsibility for your players' well-being, but lawyers recommend them.

Proper Supervision and Record Keeping

With young children, simply being present in the area of play is not enough; you must actively plan and direct team activities and closely observe and evaluate players' participation. You're the watchdog responsible for the players' well-being. So if you notice a player limping or grimacing, give him or her a rest and examine the extent of the injury.

As part of your supervision duties, you are expected to foresee potentially dangerous situations and to be in a position to help prevent them from occurring. As a coach you're required to know and enforce the rules of the sport (especially safety rules), prohibit dangerous horseplay, and hold practice or games only under safe weather conditions (see the next section). These specific supervisory activities will make the play environment safer for your players and will help protect you from liability if a mishap does occur.

As a general rule, the more dangerous an activity is, the more closely you should be supervising players. This suggests that you need to directly supervise younger, less-experienced players, especially in riskier situations, such as when they are learning new skills, are violating rules, or are tired or look unwell.

For further protection, keep records of your season plans, practice plans, and players' injuries. Season and practice plans come in handy when you need evidence that players have been taught certain skills whereas accurate, detailed injury-report forms offer protection against unfounded lawsuits. Ask for these forms from your YMCA (appendix E has a sample injury report form), and hold onto these records for several years so that an "old flag football injury" of a former player doesn't come back to haunt you.

Environmental Conditions

Most problems that arise because of environmental factors relate to excessive heat or cold, though you should also consider other environmental factors such as severe weather and pollution. Giving a little thought to potential problems and spending a little effort to ensure adequate protection for your players will prevent most serious emergencies related to environmental conditions.

Heat

On hot, humid days the body has difficulty cooling itself. Because the air is already saturated with water vapor (humidity), sweat doesn't evaporate as easily, and the body retains extra heat. Hot, humid environments make athletes prone to heat exhaustion and heatstroke (see more on these in "Providing First Aid" on page 153). And if *you* think it's hot or humid, it's harder on the kids—not just because they're more active, but because youngsters under the age of 12 have a more difficult time regulating their body temperature than adults do. To provide for players' safety in hot or humid conditions, take the following preventive measures:

- Monitor weather conditions and adjust practices and games accordingly. Figure 10.2 shows the specific air temperatures and humidity percentages that can be hazardous.
- Acclimatize players to exercising in high heat and humidity. Players can make adjustments to high heat and humidity over 7 to 10 days. During this time, hold practices and games at low-to-moderate activity levels and give the players water breaks every 20 minutes.
- Switch to light clothing. Players should wear shorts and white T-shirts.
- Identify and monitor players who are prone to heat illness. Those players who are overweight, heavily muscled, or out of shape will be more prone to heat illness, as will be those who work excessively hard or who

have suffered heat illness before. Closely monitor these players and give them water breaks every 15 to 20 minutes.

- Make sure players replace water lost through sweat. Encourage your players to drink 1 liter of water each day, to drink 8 ounces of water every 15 minutes during practice or games, and to drink 4 to 8 ounces of water 15 minutes before practice or games.
- Replenish electrolytes lost through sweat, such as sodium (salt) and potassium. The best way to replace these nutrients is by eating a normal diet that contains fresh fruits and vegetables. Bananas are a good source of potassium. The normal American diet contains plenty of salt, so players don't need to go overboard in salting their food to replace lost sodium.

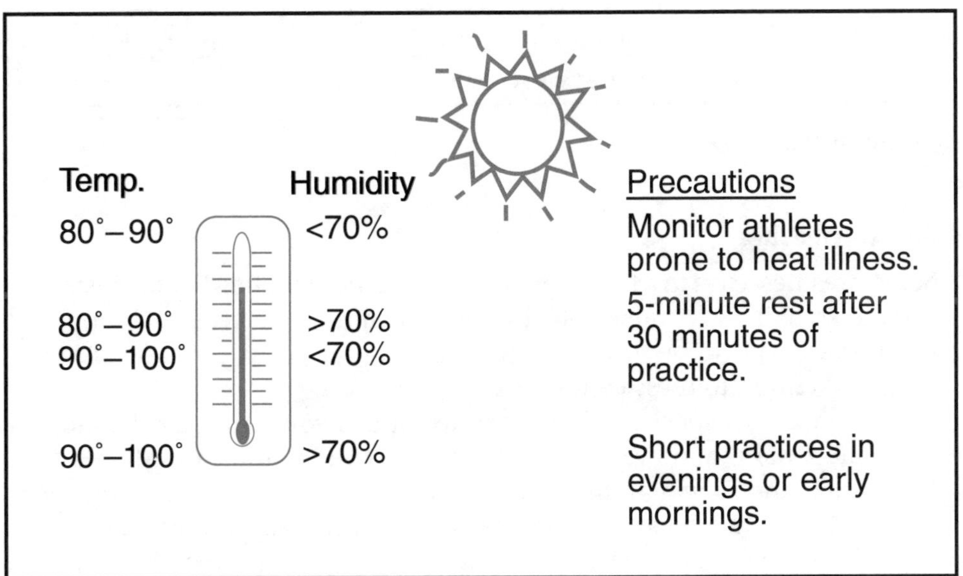

Figure 10.2 Warm-weather precautions.

Encourage players to drink plenty of water before, during, and after practice and games. Because water makes up 45 to 65 percent of a youngster's body weight and weighs about a pound per pint, the loss of even a little bit of water can have severe consequences for the body's systems. And it doesn't have to be hot and humid for players to become dehydrated. Nor do players have to feel thirsty; in fact, by the time they are aware of their thirst, they are long overdue for a drink.

Cold

When a person is exposed to cold weather, the body temperature starts to drop below normal. To counteract this, the body shivers and reduces the blood flow to gain or conserve heat. But no matter how effective the body's natural heating mechanism is, the body will better withstand cold temperatures if it is prepared to handle them. To reduce the risk of cold-related illnesses, make sure players wear appropriate protective clothing, and keep them active to maintain body heat. Also monitor the windchill (See figure 10.3).

Temperature (°F)

Wind speed (mph)	0	5	10	15	20	25	30	35	40
	Flesh may freeze within 1 minute								
40	-55	-45	-35	-30	-20	-15	-5	0	10
35	-50	-40	-35	-30	-20	-10	-5	5	10
30	-50	-40	-30	-25	-20	-10	0	5	10
25	-45	-35	-30	-20	-15	-5	0	10	15
20	-35	-30	-25	-15	-10	0	5	10	20
15	-30	-25	-20	-10	-5	0	10	15	25
10	-20	-15	-10	0	5	10	15	20	30
5	-5	0	5	10	15	20	25	30	35

Windchill temperature (°F)

Figure 10.3 Windchill index.

Severe Weather

Severe weather refers to a host of potential dangers, including lightning storms, tornadoes, hail, heavy rains (which can cause injuries by creating sloppy field conditions), and so on. If you are practicing outdoors, you will need to pay special attention to these conditions.

Lightning is of special concern because it can come up quickly and can cause great harm and even kill. For each 5-second count from the flash of lightning to the bang of thunder, lightning is 1 mile away. A flash-bang interlude of 10 seconds means the lightning is 2 miles away; an interlude of 15 seconds indicates lightning is 3 miles away. A practice or competition should be stopped for the day if lightning is 3 miles away or less (15 seconds *or less* from flash to bang).

Safe places in which to take cover when lightning strikes are fully enclosed metal vehicles with the windows up, enclosed buildings, and low ground (under cover of bushes, if possible). It's *not* safe to be near metallic objects—flag poles, fences, light poles, metal bleachers, and so on. Also avoid trees, water, and open fields.

Cancel practice or competitions when under either a tornado watch or warning. If for some reason you are playing when a tornado is nearby, you should get inside a building if possible. If not, lie in a ditch or low area, or crouch near a strong building, and use your arms to protect your head and neck.

The keys with severe weather are exercising caution and prudence. Don't try to get in that last 10 minutes of practice or a game if lightning is on the horizon. Don't continue to play in heavy rains. Many storms can strike quickly and ferociously. Respect the weather and play it safe.

Air Pollution

Poor air quality and smog can present real dangers to your players if you are practicing outdoors. Both short- and long-term lung damage are possible from participating in unsafe air. While it's true that participating in clean air is not possible in many areas, restricting activity is recommended when the air-quality ratings are worse than moderate or when there is a smog alert. Your local health department or air-quality control board can inform you of the air-quality ratings for your area and whether they recommend restricting activities.

Emergency Care

No matter how good and thorough your prevention program, injuries will occur. When an injury does strike, chances are you will be the one in charge. The severity and nature of the injury will determine how actively involved you'll be in treating the injury, but regardless of how serious the injury is, it is your responsibility to know what steps to take. So let's look at how you should prepare to provide basic emergency care to your injured players and how to take appropriate action when a minor injury or heat illness does occur.

Being Prepared

Being prepared to provide basic emergency care involves three steps: being trained in cardiopulmonary resuscitation (CPR) and first aid, having an appropriately stocked first-aid kit on hand at practices or games, and having an emergency plan.

CPR and First-Aid Training

We recommend that all YMCA Rookies coaches receive CPR and first-aid training from a nationally recognized organization (e.g., the National Safety Council, the American Heart Association, the American Red Cross, or the American Sport Education Program). You should be certified based on a practical and written test of knowledge. CPR training should include pediatric and adult basic life support and freeing of obstructed airways.

First-Aid Kit

Be sure to have a first-aid kit available at all practices and games. A well-stocked first-aid kit should include the following items:

- List of emergency phone numbers
- Change for a pay phone
- Face shield (for rescue breathing and CPR)
- Bandage scissors
- Plastic bags for crushed ice
- 3-inch and 4-inch elastic wraps
- Triangular bandages
- Sterile gauze pads—3-inch and 4-inch squares
- Saline solution for eyes
- Contact lens case
- Mirror
- Penlight
- Tongue depressors
- Cotton swabs
- Butterfly strips
- Bandage strips—assorted sizes
- Alcohol or peroxide
- Antibacterial soap
- First-aid cream or antibacterial ointment
- Petroleum jelly
- Tape adherent and tape remover
- 1 1/2-inch white athletic tape
- Prewrap
- Sterile gauze rolls
- Insect-sting kit
- Safety pins
- 1/8-inch, 1/4-inch, and 1/2-inch foam rubber
- Disposable surgical gloves
- Thermometer

Emergency Plan

An emergency plan is the final step in preparing to take appropriate action for severe or serious injuries. The plan calls for three steps:

1. **Evaluate the injured player.** Your CPR and first-aid training will guide you here.

2. **Call the appropriate medical personnel.** If possible, delegate the responsibility of seeking medical help to another calm and responsible adult who is on hand for all practices and games. Write out a list of emergency phone numbers and keep it with you. Include the following phone numbers:

   - Rescue unit
   - Hospital
   - Physician
   - Police
   - Fire department

   Take each player's emergency information to every practice and game (see appendix C). This information includes who to contact in case of an emergency, what types of medications the player is using, what types of drugs he or she is allergic to, and so on.

   Give an emergency response card (see appendix D) to the contact person calling for emergency assistance. This provides the information the contact person needs to convey and will help keep the person calm, knowing that everything he or she needs to communicate is on the card. Also complete an injury-report form (see appendix E) and keep it on file for any injury that occurs.

3. **Provide first aid.** If medical personnel are not on hand at the time of the injury, you should provide first-aid care to the extent of your qualifications. Again, while your CPR and first-aid training will guide you here, the following are important notes:

   - Do not move the injured player if (1) the injury is to the head, neck, or back; (2) a large joint (ankle, knee, elbow, shoulder) is dislocated; or (3) the pelvis, a rib, or an arm or leg is fractured.
   - Calm the injured player and keep others away from him or her as much as possible.
   - Evaluate whether the player's breathing is stopped or irregular, and, if necessary, clear the airway with your fingers.
   - Administer artificial respiration if breathing has stopped. Administer CPR if the player's circulation has stopped.
   - Remain with the player until medical personnel arrive.

Your emergency plan should follow this sequence:

1. Check the player's level of consciousness.
2. Send a contact person to call the appropriate medical personnel and to call the player's parents.

3. Send someone to wait for the rescue team and direct them to the injured player.
4. Assess the injury.
5. Administer first aid.
6. Assist emergency medical personnel in preparing the player for transportation to a medical facility.
7. Appoint someone to go with the player if the parents are not available. This person should be responsible, calm, and familiar with the player. Assistant coaches or parents are best for this job.
8. Complete an injury-report form while the incident is fresh in your mind.

Providing First Aid

Proper CPR and first-aid training, a well-stocked first-aid kit, and an emergency plan help prepare you to take appropriate action when an injury occurs. Next we'll look at how to provide first aid both for minor injuries and for heat illnesses, which can be more serious.

Keep in mind that some injuries are too severe for you to treat: head, neck, and back injuries; fractures; and injuries that cause a player to lose consciousness. In these cases you should follow the emergency plan outlined on page 150. Provide first aid *only to the extent of your qualifications.* Don't "play doctor" with injuries; sort out minor injuries that you can treat from those situations in which you need to call for assistance.

Minor Injuries

Although no injury seems minor to the player who has it, most injuries are neither life-threatening nor severe enough to restrict participation. When minor injuries occur, you can take an active role in their initial treatment. Most of the injuries you will see will be scrapes and cuts, strains and sprains, and bumps and bruises.

Scrapes and Cuts. When one of your players has an open wound, the first thing you should do is to put on a pair of disposable surgical gloves or some other effective blood barrier. Don't let a fear of acquired immune deficiency syndrome (AIDS) stop you from helping a bleeding player. You are only at risk if you allow contaminated blood to come in contact with an open wound, so the blood barrier that you wear will protect you. Check with your director or the YMCA of the USA for more information about protecting yourself and your players from AIDS.

Once you are wearing gloves, follow these four steps:

1. Stop the bleeding by applying direct pressure with a clean dressing to the wound and elevating it. The player may be able to apply this pressure while you put on your gloves. Do not remove the dressing if it becomes soaked with blood. Instead, place an additional dressing on top of the one already in place. If bleeding continues, elevate the injured area above the heart and maintain pressure.

2. Cleanse the wound thoroughly once the bleeding is controlled. A good rinsing with a forceful stream of water, and perhaps light scrubbing with soap, will help prevent infection.

3. Protect the wound with sterile gauze or a bandage. If the player continues to participate, apply protective padding over the injured area.

4. Remove the gloves and dispose of them carefully to prevent you or anyone else from coming into contact with blood.

For bloody noses not associated with serious facial injury, have the athlete sit and lean slightly forward. Then pinch the player's nostrils shut. If the bleeding continues after several minutes, or if the player has a history of nosebleeds, seek medical assistance.

Strains and Sprains. The physical demands of playing often result in injury to the muscles or tendons (strains) or to the ligaments (sprains). When your players suffer minor strains or sprains, immediately apply the PRICE method of injury care (see figure 10.4):

P Protect the player and injured body part from further danger or trauma.

R Rest the area to avoid further damage and to also foster healing.

I Ice the area to reduce swelling and pain.

C Compress the area by securing an ice bag in place with an elastic wrap.

E Elevate the injury above heart level to keep the blood from pooling in the area.

Figure 10.4 The PRICE method.

Bumps and Bruises. Inevitably players make contact with each other and with the ground. If the force of a body part at impact is great enough, a bump or bruise will result. Many players continue playing with such sore spots, but if the bump or bruise is large and painful, you should act appropriately. Use the PRICE method of injury care and monitor the injury. If swelling, discoloration, and pain have lessened, the player may resume participation with protective padding; if not, the player should be examined by a physician.

Heat Illnesses

In case your team ever must play under hot conditions, you also should know how to handle two types of heat illnesses: heat exhaustion and heatstroke.

Heat Exhaustion. Heat exhaustion is a shock-like condition caused by dehydration and electrolyte depletion. Symptoms include headache, nausea, dizziness, chills, fatigue, and extreme thirst (see figure 10.5 for heat exhaustion and heatstroke symptoms). Signs include pale, cool, and clammy skin; rapid, weak pulse; loss of coordination; dilated pupils; and profuse sweating (this is a key sign).

A player suffering from heat exhaustion should rest in a cool, shaded area; drink cool water; and have ice applied to the neck, back, or stomach to help cool the body. You may have to administer CPR if necessary or send for emergency medical assistance if the player doesn't recover or if his or her condition worsens. Under no condition should the player return to activity that day or before he or she regains all the weight lost through sweat. If the player had to see a physician, he or she shouldn't return to practice until released by the physician.

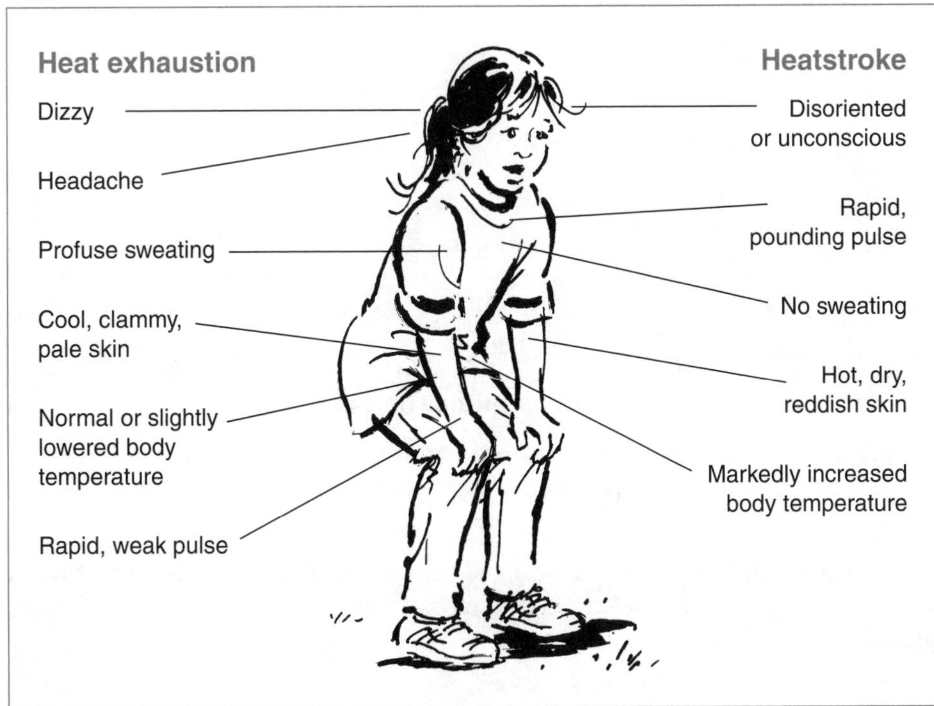

Figure 10.5 Heat exhaustion vs. heat stroke.

Heatstroke. Heatstroke is a life-threatening condition in which the body *stops* sweating and body temperature rises dangerously high. It occurs when dehydration causes a malfunction in the body's temperature control center in the brain. Symptoms include the feeling of being on fire (extremely hot), nausea, confusion, irritability, and fatigue. Signs include hot, dry, and flushed or red skin (this is a key sign); lack of sweat; rapid pulse; rapid breathing; constricted pupils; vomiting; diarrhea; and possibly seizures, unconsciousness, or respiratory or cardiac arrest. See figure 10.5 for heat exhaustion and heatstroke symptoms.

Send for emergency medical assistance immediately and have the player rest in a cool, shaded area. Remove excess clothing and equipment on the player, and cool his or her body with cool, wet towels or by pouring cool water over him or her. Apply ice packs to the armpits, neck, back, stomach, and between the legs. If the player is conscious, have him or her drink cool water. If the player is unconscious, place the player on his or her side to allow fluids and vomit to drain from the mouth.

A player who has suffered heatstroke can't return to practice until he or she is released by a physician.

Legal Liability

When one of your players is injured, naturally your first concern is his or her well-being. Your feelings for children, after all, are what made you decide to coach. Unfortunately there is something else that you must consider: Can you be held liable for the injury?

From a legal standpoint, a coach has nine duties to fulfill. In this chapter we've discussed all of them except planning (see chapters 5-7 on appropriate plans).

1. Provide a safe environment.
2. Properly plan the activity.
3. Provide adequate and proper equipment.
4. Match or equate athletes.
5. Warn of inherent risks in the sport.
6. Supervise the activity closely.
7. Evaluate athletes for injury or incapacitation.
8. Know emergency procedures and first aid.
9. Keep adequate records.

In addition to fulfilling these nine legal duties, you should check your YMCA's insurance coverage and your own personal coverage to make sure you are protected from liability.

chapter 11

Teaching Character Development

This final chapter deals with character development, the teaching of values to players. At the YMCA, teaching values is as important a part of the flag football program as is teaching game skills. As a YMCA coach, you take on the responsibility to help children learn about and use four core values, the values that the YMCA has chosen to emphasize: caring, honesty, respect, and responsibility. Here are just some of the ways you can do this:

- Communicate to your players that good sportsmanship is an important part of the program.
- Teach the four values to players so they know what those values mean. Give them examples.
- Include the values in each practice session (character development discussions appear in each practice plan).
- Consistently model the values in your own behavior so players can see what those values look like.
- Celebrate the values and hold them up to players as what is right in order to help them learn to believe in those values.

- Ask players to practice the values, over and over again.
- Consistently reinforce and reward behaviors that support the values, using the specific value word that is relevant: "Cindy, thanks for helping Amy pick up the cones. That shows caring."
- Consistently confront a player whose behavior is inconsistent with the values, but do so in a way that does not devalue him or her.
- Be prepared to talk with parents about the character development portion of the program.

Teaching players values takes a somewhat different approach than teaching skills:

- First, it requires that you yourself be a good role model. You should set an example with your words and actions.
- Second, you need to understand at what level your players are capable of understanding and applying values. Younger children do not think about moral decisions in the same way as adults. Children gradually develop the ability to understand values as they grow.
- Third, you need to learn to identify situations during practice that relate to the four values. Many everyday occurrences provide a chance for you to demonstrate to players that values are relevant to their daily lives.
- Finally, use the Team Circle discussions suggested in the practice plans or find activities of your own, ones that emphasize values and make players think about them.

Being a Good Role Model

Most of us believe in the YMCA's core values of caring, honesty, respect, and responsibility, but we don't always follow our own beliefs. Our character is determined by our behavior. We judge our character by our good intentions. Other people judge us only by our behavior. Consider the following lists of sample coaching behaviors for each value. These aren't meant to be comprehensive lists; they're intended to get you thinking about what it means, in practical terms, to be a good role model as it applies to these four important values.

Caring

- You spend time after practice helping a player learn a skill.
- You comfort a player who is dejected after a loss.
- You help a player who is stressed manage that stress.
- You inform your players of the benefits of good nutrition.

Honesty

- You tell a player that she's not executing a skill correctly and you'll help her.

- You tell a player when you don't know a rule (but you'll find out what it is).
- You tell a player when you make a mistake, such as misinterpreting who instigated minor misbehavior during practice.
- You tell your team that you haven't been as physically active in the off-season as you'd like to be, but you're trying to improve.

Respect

- You don't blow your cool when players misbehave.
- You listen to players attentively when they are talking.
- You bring the same energy and enthusiasm for teaching skills to all your players, no matter how skilled they are.
- You don't criticize players in front of their teammates.

Responsibility

- You show up on time and prepared for all practices and contests.
- You provide appropriate first aid for injured players.
- You closely supervise all practice activities.
- You intervene when players are misbehaving.

Understanding Children's Moral Reasoning

As you work with children on character development, keep in mind how they think about moral questions. They approach such questions much differently than an adult would, and their perspectives change as they grow. One researcher, Kohlberg, has developed a set of stages for thinking about moral questions (Bee 1995; Crain 1992) that he believes children move through as they mature.

Children up through the age of nine usually think about moral questions in terms of obedience and punishment. They assume that fixed rules are set by powerful adults who can enforce those rules by punishment. Children are doing right when they obey the rules unquestioningly. Actions are judged by their outcomes, not by the person's intentions.

Moral reasoning for children nine years and younger is very "black and white." In flag football, you might expect to see children interpret being tripped by an opponent *personally*—as an intentional attack—when it is most likely unintentional and a result of poor skill or lack of experience.

Around the age of 10, most children think about moral questions in terms of what works best for them. The right thing is the thing that brings pleasant results. They also think about making deals with others: if I do something for you, then you may in turn do something for me. Making fair deals is important. A 10- or 11-year-old may agree to congratulate the opponent on good plays or at the end of a game because he or she knows that the behavior pleases most adults and most other kids. However, if the individual's opponent doesn't congratulate his or her good play in return, the child may stop that behavior because it doesn't generate a pleasant or "fair" result.

By about 16 years, most players have started thinking about moral questions in terms of how those questions relate to the expectations of their family and community. The key focus is behaving in good ways and having good motives and good feelings toward others. At this point, too, players start taking into account people's *intentions* when judging actions.

They can better understand their roles as representatives of their team or their YMCA and as role models for younger players. This is particularly true when their coaches, parents, and teammates encourage them in this direction. Such encouragement would be likely to cause them to modify their game behaviors to fulfill others' expectations.

Moving from one type of thinking about morality to another happens gradually, and may occur at different ages for different children. However, this gives you some broad guidelines for how the majority of the players on your team may look at character development when you bring such questions up in Team Circles or during practice or games.

Using "Teachable" Moments

During practices, you may find that a situation arises that gives you a chance to point out how values apply. This type of situation is known as a *teachable moment,* and it might be something like one team's behavior toward an opponent, one player's behavior toward another, or a violation of team rules. Use teachable moments when they occur. Stop a drill or game to comment on an incident. It's best to avoid doing this too frequently. Used appropriately, when a good opportunity arises to illustrate a value you've discussed earlier, this teaching technique can be highly effective.

A teachable moment can be triggered by either good or bad actions; you can praise an individual's or group's supportive, fair behavior or stop an activity briefly to talk about negative behavior. Here are some examples:

- If one player yells at another for a mistake in play, talk to that player about respect.
- If a player does something dangerous during a game, have a brief discussion with that player about responsibility and caring for others.
- If a player helps another child who is hurt, praise the player for being caring.
- If a player raises her hand to admit committing a foul that wasn't called, congratulate her for being honest.

Try to balance positive and negative instances; don't use just negative situations as teachable moments.

In summary, teachable moments are occasions when you can hold up the right value and explain why some behavior is the acceptable thing to do.

Doing this illustrates to players what values look like, beyond the words, and how values are a part of our everyday lives.

 Using Values Activities

We've already included a Team Circle in each practice plan. This gives you a topic for brief discussion of one or more of the core values. Just as practice drills focus on physical skills, Team Circles focus on character development. They help players realize that participation in flag football also teaches them about themselves and others.

Here are some tips on leading Team Circle discussions:

- Begin discussions by reviewing the YMCA House Rules: speak for yourself, listen to others, avoid put-downs, take charge of yourself, and show respect. (Repeat this in your first three or four Team Circles; after that, you'll probably only need to reinforce these House Rules occasionally.)
- Be yourself. Children respect an adult who listens to them and who talks honestly.
- As a role model for your players, be willing to admit mistakes; it will make players more likely to be open about themselves.
- Give players a chance to respond, but allow them to pass if they want to. Reinforce their responses with a nod, smile, or short comment like "Thanks," "OK," "That's interesting," or "I understand." Give the player speaking your undivided attention.
- After all players have had a chance to respond to your Team Circle question, briefly summarize the responses and add your own comments. Try not to lecture.

You might also include activities of your own that reinforce values. The YMCA of the USA has created a number of character development resources; ask your YMCA Youth Super Sports Director if he or she can make those available to you. Here are a few ideas taken from the YMCA *Character Development Activity Box:*

- Tell your players that one way to demonstrate caring is to do kind things for others. Ask the players to brainstorm ideas of things they could do to be kind to the other members of their families. Some ideas might be washing dishes, cleaning their rooms, or telling a story to a younger brother or sister. Encourage each player to do one kind act for each member of his or her family during the next week, and discuss what they did during the next week's practice.

- Point out that on a team all players must respect their teammates, because they are not a team without every one of them. Divide the team into two equal groups. Have each group line up in single file as fast as it can in the order you tell the members to. They can race to see which group can line up the fastest. First say, "I want you to line up from shortest to tallest." After both groups have done that, indicate who won and congratulate both groups. Then say, "Now line up by birthday month, with January in the front and December in the back." Next say, "Line up by biggest foot to smallest." Finish by saying, "OK, everybody have a seat back in the circle." Ask, "Now, in that game, who were the most important players: the short ones or the tall ones? That's right—all were equally important. The same is true for when you were born or how big your foot is. The fact is that every person is important on a team and worthy of your respect. Teamwork is when everyone does his or her part, no matter what that is or how much attention it gets."

- Discuss with your players the idea of "cooperation" versus "competition." Point out that the other team makes the game possible. Ask the players to brainstorm ways they might show respect to the other team. These might include saying positive things to the opposing players, congratulating them for outstanding plays, and shaking hands at the end of a game. Encourage your players to do these things when they play.

Any activities you use should meet these criteria:

- Be age-appropriate and developmentally appropriate.
- Account for varied personal backgrounds and differing views on values.
- Attempt to change players' attitudes as well as their actions.
- Focus on long-term results.
- Be planned and intentional.
- Fit logically with what you are doing.
- Be positive and constructive, not putting players down.
- Be inclusive.
- Be meaningful, not trivial or corny.
- Be fun!

Finding More Information

Videos

The Official Pop Warner Football Video Handbook. Available through Amazon.com. The video provides offensive drills on receiving, blocking, and passing and provides advice on defensive sets, line pursuit, and strategy.

Youth Football Strategies for Success. Available through Amazon.com. Guides coaches through various offensive and defensive strategies in preparing their players for success.

Organizations

United States Flag & Touch Football League
7709 Ohio St.
Mentor, OH 44060
(440) 974-8735

American Flag and Touch Football League
P.O. Box 518
Bethpage, NY 11714
(516) 822-6312

Preparticipation Screening for YMCA Youth Super Sports Programs

A Statement of the YMCA of the USA Medical Advisory Committee

The YMCA believes in providing a safe experience for all youth participating in YMCA sports programs. Although staff and other program leaders are primarily responsible for the health and safety of the children during training and competition, it is equally important for parents to determine that their children participating in YMCA sports have no medical conditions that would preclude their participation or result in further injury or harm.

The YMCA of the USA Medical Advisory Committee recommends that YMCAs encourage parents of youth participating in YMCA sports programs to have their children screened for the purpose of (1) determining the general health of the child, (2) detecting medical or musculoskeletal conditions that may predispose a child to injury or illness during competition, and (3) detecting potentially life-threatening or disabling conditions that may limit a child's participation. The following 10 questions are particularly important for a physician to ask during a sports preparticipation exam[1]:

1. Have you ever passed out during or after exercise?
2. Have you ever been dizzy during or after exercise?
3. Have you ever had chest pain during or after exercise?
4. Do you get tired more quickly than your friends do during exercise?
5. Have you ever had racing of your heart or skipped heartbeats?
6. Have you ever had high blood pressure or high cholesterol?
7. Have you ever been told you have a heart murmur?
8. Has any family member or relative died of heart problems or a sudden death before age 50?
9. Have you had a severe viral infection (for example, myocarditis or mononucleosis) within the last month?
10. Has a physician ever denied or restricted your participation in sports for any heart problems?

Although not a complete list, these questions address the most likely areas of concern and are helpful in identifying individuals at high risk. A "yes" answer to any question should result in further evaluation and a discussion between physician and parent about appropriate sport participation for the child.

On the registration form for each youth sports program, there should be a statement requiring a parent's or guardian's signature, indicating that the child has been properly screened and there are no medical conditions or injuries precluding his or her participation in that sport.

---

[1] *Preparticipation Physical Evaluation,* Second Edition, American Academy of Family Physicians, American Academy of Pediatrics, American Medical Society for Sports Medicine, American Orthopaedic Society for Sports Medicine, American Osteopathic Academy of Sports Medicine, 1997.

Emergency Information Card

Athlete's name ____________________ Age ______
Address ____________________
Phone ____________________ S.S.# ____________________
Sport ____________________

List two persons to contact in case of emergency:

Parent or guardian's name ____________________ Home phone __________
Address ____________________ Work phone __________

Second person's name ____________________ Home phone __________
Address ____________________ Work phone __________
Relationship to athlete ____________________

Insurance co. ____________________ Policy # __________
Physician's name ____________________ Phone __________

IMPORTANT

Is your child allergic to any drugs? ______ If so, what? ____________________
Does your child have any other allergies? (e.g., bee stings, dust) __________
Does your child suffer from ____ asthma, ____ diabetes, or ____ epilepsy? (Check any that apply.)
Is your child on any medication? ______ If so, what? ____________________

Does your child wear contacts? ______

Is there anything else we should know about your child's health or physical condition? If yes, please explain. ____________________

Signature ____________________ Date __________

Emergency Response Card

Information for Emergency Call (be prepared to give this information to the EMS dispatcher)

1. Location ____________________
   Street address ____________________
   City or town ____________________
   Directions (cross streets, landmarks, etc.) ____________________
   ____
2. Telephone number from which the call is being made ____________________
3. Caller's name ____________________
4. What happened ____________________
   ____
   ____
   ____
   ____
   ____
5. How many persons injured ____________________
6. Condition of victim(s) ____________________
7. Help (first aid) being given ____________________

Note: Do not hang up first. Let the EMS dispatcher hang up first.

Injury Report

Name of athlete ______________________________

Date ______________________________

Time ______________________________

First aider (name) ______________________________

Cause of injury ______________________________

____

Type of injury ______________________________

Anatomical area involved ______________________________

Extent of injury ______________________________

First aid administered ______________________________

____

Other treatment administered ______________________________

____

____

Referral action ______________________________

____

____

First aider (signature)

Resources and Suggested Readings

American Sport Education Program. 1997. *Coaching youth football.* 2nd ed. Champaign, IL: Human Kinetics.

Bee, Helen. 1995. *The developing child.* 7th ed. New York: HarperCollins College Publishers.

Berk, Laura E. 1998. *Development through the lifespan.* Needham Heights, MA: Allyn & Bacon.

Crain, William. 1992. *Theories of development: Concepts and applications.* 3rd ed. Englewood Cliffs, NJ: Prentice Hall.

Flegel, Melinda J. 1997. *Sport first aid.* Updated edition. Champaign, IL: Human Kinetics.

Humphrey, James H. 1993. *Sports for children: A guide for adults.* Springfield, IL: Charles C Thomas.

Kalish, Susan. 1996. *Your child's fitness: Practical advice for parents.* Champaign, IL: Human Kinetics.

YMCA of the USA. 1997. *Character development activity box.* Chicago: YMCA of the USA.

YMCA of the USA. 1999. *YMCA youth fitness program.* Champaign, IL: Human Kinetics.